THE WAY OF NATURAL HISTORY

THE WAY OF NATURAL HISTORY

EDITED BY THOMAS LOWE FLEISCHNER

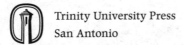
Trinity University Press
San Antonio

Published by Trinity University Press
San Antonio, Texas 78212

Copyright © 2011 by Thomas Lowe Fleischner

"The Supple Deer," copyright © 2008 by Jane Hirschfield
"Mind in the Forest," copyright © 2009 by Scott Russell Sanders

Cover design by Nicole Hayward
Book design by BookMatters, Berkeley

Trinity University Press strives to produce its books using methods and materials in an environmentally sensitive manner. We favor working with manufacturers that practice sustainable management of all natural resources, produce paper using recycled stock, and manage forests with the best possible practices for people, biodiversity, and sustainability. The press is a member of the Green Press Initiative, a nonprofit program dedicated to supporting publishers in their efforts to reduce their impacts on endangered forests, climate change, and forest dependent communities.

The paper used in this publication meets the minimum requirements of the American National Standard for Information Sciences—Permanence of Paper for Printed Library Materials, ANSI Z39.48-1992.

Library of Congress Cataloging-in-Publication Data

The way of natural history / [edited by] Thomas Lowe Fleischner.
    p. cm.
   Summary: "Scientists, nature writers, poets, and Zen practitioners highlight their individual ways of paying attention to nature and discuss how their experiences have enlivened and enhanced their worlds. The essays provide models for interacting with the natural world and create a call for the importance of natural history as a discipline"—Provided by publisher.
   ISBN 978-1-59534-073-3 (hardback) — ISBN 978-1-59534-074-0 (paperback)
    1. Natural history.   2. Naturalists.   3. Nature study.   4. Natural history—Philosophy.   I. Fleischner, Thomas Lowe, 1954—
   QH81.W387 2011
   509.2'2—dc22   2011001294

15   14   13   12   11 | 5   4   3   2   1

Contents

The Supple Deer

The quiet opening
between fence strands
perhaps eighteen inches.

Antlers to hind hooves,
four feet off the ground,
the deer poured through it.

No tuft of the coarse white belly hair left behind.

I don't know how a stag turns
into a stream of water.
I have never felt such accurate envy.

Not of the deer.

To be that porous, to have such largeness pass through me.

The Mindfulness of Natural History

From here, the tropical forest stretches more than two thousand miles toward the Atlantic coast. In the sticky heat I walk beside the Rio Puyo, along the uppermost edge of the Ecuadorian Amazon, having just descended from the Andean highlands. There's a tingling sense that something new, something beautiful, might manifest at any moment, around any corner. The flick of a leaf, the chip-note of an unseen bird—these are potential portals into new worlds. This sense of total alertness enlivens me; the air throbs, ready to explode, it seems, into new life forms. Across the muddy river, a rustle among the treetops seizes my attention, then there it is: a finch-sized bird with a luminescent turquoise head, sharply contrasting with a black body, splashed with a straw-yellow patch on its wing. A bird so gaudy and brilliant, I laugh aloud. In the next moment, a second bird, about the same size, flies onto the next branch, so close it's visible in the same binocular view. This bird shimmers lime-green, with a lemon-yellow belly. They both jounce the branches a bit as they grab insects, then fly off, deeper into the forest. I grab my field guide—the monumental *Birds of Ecuador*, which, given the tremendous diversity of this biologically blessed nation, fills my shoulder bag. Because of their size, behavior, and fanciful coloration, I'm pretty sure these are both tanagers—members of a large tropical family of fruit-eating birds. Soon I've narrowed it down: a blue-necked tanager (I must concur with the field guide authors' enthusiasm: "arguably one of the more stunning members in a wonderful genus") and a female swallow tanager. My actual observation of these two lasted only half a minute, but weeks later I still tingle with the memory, and with the knowledge that creatures such as these are out there, going about their business, each and every moment of each and every day.

Another morning, far to the south. Low-angle sun of the austral summer glints off the surface of the violet-blue bay, whitecaps kicking up spray into the steady twenty-knot wind. But here on shore, more than two hundred thousand birds stand erect, each as tall as my waist, squawking up a collective cacophony that can be heard well out to sea—almost as far as the fertile scent of their guano can be smelled. Most of these king penguins are in full adult plumage: gleaming white breasts, with charcoal-gray heads, necklaced with sun-bright yellow, the same color that forms a teardrop patch on each side of their heads, like golden exclamation points on each bird. Scattered throughout the colony are the juveniles, which have a completely different appearance—shaggy and uniformly brown. These adolescents cluster together in small pockets, readying themselves to overwinter on this sub-Antarctic island. All in all, these are stunning creatures. Even a single bird would be astonishing, but so many thousands, packed within a body length of one another, together filling an entire valley, is almost incomprehensible, beyond my senses' ability to process. This enormous colony—the center of the world for this species—is severed into halves by the gracious curves of a river, pulsing with fresh glacial meltwater, its source visible in the daunting, jagged peaks that jut almost three thousand meters above this remote beach in the Southern Ocean. As an early explorer exclaimed on encountering this island: "It's like coming upon the Alps in the middle of the ocean."

As I move away from the fringe of the penguin colony, Antarctic fur seals glare at me, corkscrewing their necks in broad circles and snapping their formidable teeth in warning. Occasionally I have to waggle a slender stick in their direction to discourage those jaws from chomping onto my leg. Amid all this swarming life, three hours pass by in a blur, and soon it's time to load back into our rubber landing boats and bounce across the roughening sea to our ship.

And the most important moment: this one. Right now, right here. Early spring sun casting broad shadows, glinting bright copper in large patches on the pine needle forest floor. The wind from the end of the huge cyclonic storm system spinning east is almost past us now. Yet the wind's whipping tail tosses the tops of ponderosa pines as if they were cornstalks on the prairie, their long needles twirling against azure sky. The sound of the powerful wind burrows through the trees, shouldering away the spring sounds of finches. My eyes flick from golden grama grass waving in the sunlit openings to glossy-green Emory oak leaves mirroring the sun. My ears trace the crescendo and decrescendo of wind. My imagination feels the snowmelt moisture slowly percolating into volcanic soil beneath my crossed legs. I'm no longer alone in the world. Rather, I've connected with my true neighbors, and with the force that flows along the ribs of the continent.

Natural history is a practice of intentional, focused attentiveness and receptivity to the more-than-human world, guided by honesty and accuracy. Simply put, it is paying attention to the bigger world outside our own heads. As Zen Rōshi (and contributor to this volume) Robert Aitken noted, attention is prerequisite to intimacy. Natural history, then, is a means of becoming intimate with the big, wild world. For some, this involves watching birds visit a feeder outside a city apartment. For others, it's an annual pilgrimage to witness the spring bloom of desert flowers. Flyfishers pay close attention to aquatic insect larvae, snorkelers gain joy watching the synchronized movements of reef fishes, and geologists trace the evolution of the Earth by following bends and folds in sedimentary rocks. The mind of a hunter is nothing if not attentive to nuances of animal movement and color. With some 30 million species living on this remarkable planet, across an endless variety of landscapes, and interacting in an infinite number of ways, there is literally no limit to the "nature" we can pay attention to.

Mindfulness, a crucial element of many spiritual lineages, is particularly closely allied with Buddhist traditions, which include it as one of the elements of the Noble Eightfold Path. Right Mindfulness involves cultivating a state of increasing clarity and intensity of consciousness, one that filters out illusions and projections. Recognition of the importance of focused attentiveness is common to most spiritual traditions. Christian monks spend long hours in contemplative silence, Hindu yogis focus their minds through breathing and body movements, Sufi dancers invoke unity with the divine, Tibetans chant sutras. By whatever name—mindfulness, meditation, prayer, zazen, contemplation—a process of quieting the mind and attending to the unadorned particularities of the world has been deemed an essential component of human spiritual endeavor across cultures, languages, continents, and time.

Buddhist scholar Nyanaponika Thera, in *The Heart of Bud-*

dhist Meditation, notes that mindfulness begins with a "taking notice," a "turning toward" an object (or, one could extrapolate— a bird, a flower, a dragonfly . . .). Thich Nhat Hanh declared that "mindfulness is the foundation of a happy life" and that practicing it helps us "become a real person." Poet (and contributor to this volume) Jane Hirshfield has noted that "in a state of open mindfulness, a broad subliminal attention is going out in many directions at once." In short, mindfulness represents the mind on full alert, open to sensation and stimuli, eager to engage. Recently, psychologists have developed a keen interest in mindfulness due to its role in helping people maintain psychic balance and health. Shinzen Young, a Buddhist teacher, asserts that mindfulness training leads to greater clarity and equanimity, which he suggests are analogous to strength and flexibility in physical fitness training. In the last few years a professional literature on mindfulness has sprouted. The gist of these articles, largely buried in technical psychology journals, is that mindfulness revolves around openness to present-moment experiences. Such openness, say the psychologists, leads to acceptance and nonjudgment. As Buddhist teachers have long taught, enlightenment derives from full awareness of each present moment.

Natural history and mindfulness are two surfaces of the same leaf, a seamless merging of attentiveness outward and inward, toward the interwoven realms of nature and psyche. For some people, the window is clearer looking outward; for others, it's easier to look within. But regardless of what is being attended, the practice of mindful attention is very much the same, and the two practices are fully complementary. That Gautama, the historical Buddha, had his original moment of awakening while seated under a tree is probably not coincidental.

Mindfulness practices of all traditions share three characteristics: a commitment to developing the capacity to pay attention; an object or ally to pay attention to (typically, one's breath); and a focus on in-the-body rather than out-of-body experience. The first notion—developing skill at paying attention—is fully concordant with any definition of natural history. But some advocates of mindfulness have concentrated on the importance of interior reality, while neglecting that which occurs outside. When considering mindfulness, we should erase the false boundary between inwardly and outwardly directed attention. Jungian psychologist James Hillman has pointed out that "the cut" between "the me" and "the other" is completely arbitrary. (In fact, he asserts that psychology's core issue should be examining the uncertainty of this boundary.) Recognition of the essential permeability of the "self" and larger "ecological self" leads to a sense of unity between mindful practices directed toward the inner and outer landscapes. Hillman concluded that "the most profoundly collective and unconscious self is the natural material world."

As I sit in the forest, legs crossed, attention to my breathing encourages awareness of rhythms inside the boundary of my skin. Noticing grosbeaks sing from the upper branches of pines catalyzes a sense of "a psyche the size of earth" (to use Hillman's phrase). And attentiveness to the melodious song emphasizes the fuzziness of the boundary between inner and outer: Does the sound emanate from the bird's syrinx or as vibrations upon my eardrum? Or is this sensation really about the merging of the two?

Fully developed attentiveness toward the natural world is nothing new. Human ecologist Paul Shepard asserted that the very nature of human consciousness—the way our brains developed capacities for paying attention—is a result of our keen attentiveness toward predators and prey while evolving from other primates. "Animals," he wrote, "are among the first inhabitants of the mind's eye. They are basic to the development of speech and thought . . . indispensable to our becoming human in the fullest sense." Millennia before "mindfulness" or "natural history" emerged as concepts, our human ancestors paid close heed to interior and exterior worlds and the ways they interpenetrated.

Why does attentiveness to nature matter? In a very fundamental sense, we *are* what we pay attention to. Paying heed to beauty, grace, and everyday miracles promotes a sense of possibility and coherence that runs deeper and truer than the often illusory commercial, social "realities" advanced by mainstream contemporary culture. Even awareness of the grimmer sides of nature (predation, death, decay), when witnessed in ecological context, illuminates the essence and poignancy of human potential.

Our attention is precious, and what we choose to focus it on has enormous consequences. What we choose to look at, to listen to—these choices change the world. As Thich Nhat Hanh has pointed out, we *become* the bad television programs that we watch. A society that expends its energies tracking the latest doings of the current celebrity couple is fundamentally distinct from one that watches for the first arriving spring migrant birds, or takes a weekend to check out insects in a mountain stream, or looks inside flowers to admire the marvelous ingenuities involved in pollination. The former tends to drag culture down to its lowest commonalities; the latter can lift us up in a sense of unity with all life.

John Tarrant, a Zen Buddhist teacher and psychologist, noted that "attention is the most basic form of love"—a form of blessing. Nicolas Malebranche, a French philosopher in the seventeenth and eighteenth centuries, said that "attentiveness is the natural prayer of the soul." And, indeed, my own observation over three decades of teaching natural history is that it routinely has a centering, uplifting effect on people. Among the attributes I've noticed in those who are attentive to nature are a greater sense of humility, affirmation, hope, and gratitude. At the end of a natural history outing, jaws often ache from smiling—there's so much joy, so much laughter. Who among us can't stand some of this tonic? Paying careful attention to life is, unsurprisingly, life-affirming. Natural history tends to lead to an expanded sense of a naturalist's own humanity.

Natural history is the oldest continuous human tradition. Throughout history attentiveness to nature was so completely entwined with daily life and survival that it was never considered as a practice separate from life itself. In modern life, though, most people have become distanced from the kind of direct interaction with other patterns and processes of life and other living beings—other presences—that was formerly taken for granted. Simply put, there has never been a moment in the story of human existence when natural history was practiced so little.

Our current lack of consideration of what poet W. S. Merwin refers to as "the unrepeatable world"—the massive, unique creation we know as nature—reveals a fundamental hubris in modern life. This lack of attentiveness to nature correlates with a plethora of social, cultural, and environmental maladies: widespread depression, violence, and pollution. Why is there a correlation? Because attentiveness to the more expansive consciousness of "nature" inherently promotes humility and questioning; the lack of it can promote smugness.

Yet alienation from nature is becoming more widespread.

Attention to nature has been marginalized in many institutions. A great many universities have replaced teachers of field natural history with molecular biology researchers. In the realm of K–12 education these days, it takes real commitment to devote a single week out of thirteen years of schooling to field-based environmental education. Many school systems are cutting out even simple field trips, in part due to concerns about safety and litigation. In his *Last Child in the Woods*, Richard Louv notes that modern society teaches young people to avoid direct experience in nature. He coined the phrase "nature deficit disorder" to describe the resulting syndrome of dysfunction. Recent behavioral research makes clear that decreases in direct interactions with nature correlate closely with more indoor sedentary recreation involving electronic media (an increase in "videophilia"). Other recent research verifies that the sense of psychological well-being among urban dwellers reflects the degree of biological diversity they encounter—people simply feel better when surrounded by a diversity of plants and animals.

Even indoor sedentary connection to the natural world is being systematically eliminated. Recently the editors of the *Oxford Junior Encyclopedia* announced that they were removing a great many nature words (buttercup, acorn, fern, wren, and the like) and replacing them with currently fashionable words from technology (broadband, voice mail, database, and so on). So in the lexicon of young people, BlackBerry the electronic gadget replaces blackberry the luscious fruit. With what language will these people discover and express their innate affinity for the rest of creation—that fundamental human tendency that E. O. Wilson termed "biophilia"?

But the simple, elegant practice of natural history—which every person is wired to do, and which costs almost nothing—helps us fall in love outwardly with the world. Natural history

attentiveness was the source of the earliest human literature—
stories of the day's hunt vigorously acted out around campfires—and our first art, whether the cave paintings at Lascaux
or petroglyphs chiseled into the desert-varnished sandstone
canyons of the Colorado Plateau. As Joseph Campbell, among
others, pointed out, we owe the very forms of our bodies and
the structures of our minds to the natural history–infused lifeways of our Paleolithic forebears. Prioritizing a reconnection
with such fundamental elements of our original mind—paying
attention to the larger forces we are a part of—will be crucial
to finding a pathway toward environmental sustainability and
interpersonal sanity.

If the predilection toward natural history is so fundamentally
innate to *Homo sapiens*, why have we strayed so far from it?
Have modern humans simply outgrown the need for outwardly
directed attentiveness? And what of those people in crowded
cities or in poorer, less developed parts of the world? Is natural history simply a luxury, an artifact of a privileged colonial
mindset?

Is it more challenging to find "nature" to attend in big cities?
Often, yes—but far from impossible. For one thing, "vacant lot"
is one of the greatest of urban misnomers—for even small open
spaces in cities harbor patches of wildness well worth examining. Tiny flowers emerge from cracked pavement; butterflies
come sip their nectar. Curbside trees green up in spring; insects
hatch from tiny eggs hidden in crevices along the branches;
birds soon descend to forage in this reborn biological exuber-
ance. Moreover, many great cities have parks and other green
spaces that can concentrate wildlife. New York's Central Park
and Boston's Mount Auburn Cemetery, to cite just two exam-

ples, are famously spectacular sites to witness the spring song-bird migration.

There is no reason to believe that poverty-stricken regions of the globe are less inclined to engage in natural history, for there is no direct relationship between economic hardship and lack of interest in the natural world. In fact, often the opposite is true: Campesinos living close to the bone often live close to the land. Indeed, many peasants, fisher folk, and forest dwellers still actively utilize their natural history field skills to supplement their kitchens and their medicine shelves with wild plants and animals. Some of the best naturalists I've ever met have been people living off the bottom end of any economic development concept of poverty, whether indigenous hunter-gatherers along desert seacoasts of Mexico, sheepherders high in the Andes, or homesteaders in Pacific Northwest river valleys.

Paying attention to the more-than-human world can be irrelevant only to the extent that clarity of mind and connection with and understanding of greater forces are no longer relevant, to the extent that humility and joy no longer serve the human spirit. Marginalized peoples, whether in sprawling cities or desolate backcountry, need the psychological gifts provided by mindful natural history as much as, if not more than, any academic, museum-going sophisticate.

Natural history is not a privilege, but a right—a fundamental capacity and need of all people. And because its practice requires no fancy tools or technology, it is easily available. Indeed, one of the causes of its demise in many institutional settings—not least academia—is that little money need be exchanged for natural history to be fostered. We don't need gas chromatographs, mass spectrometers, fancy laboratories. We can do this work with our bare hands.

Natural history mindfulness offers many gifts—glimpses of wholeness, connection, and beauty that continue to teach, inspire, and heal for many years.

Along the Escalante River, scarlet flowers bloom on copper-sand terraces under cottonwoods and box elders, while black-headed grosbeaks sing their long, up-and-down song from hidden branches. Pausing to peer through a hand lens into the tubular cathedral of a *Penstemon* flower, I'm startled by the remarkable array of golden hairs, and the precise seam in each anther, about to burst with pollen.

In the Cascades, five-hundred-year-old Douglas-firs reach into the clouds, which dump silent, steady rain. Higher up, the smell of soil just emerging from a nine-month winter, yellow glacier lilies blooming right at the snowmelt edge, anxious for the fleeting summer to begin. The sharp whistle of a marmot piercing the stillness, then the wind bringing chill.

In the Sea of Cortez, I'm roused each time I step inside an open boat, for I know that one-third of the world's whale and dolphin species lunge through these food-rich waters, and the richest concentration of seabirds south of Alaska clusters on sea cliffs. The pulse of possibilities: gatherings of fin whales heaving their immense bodies through dense schools of plankton; Craveri's murrelet, one of the least-known birds in North America, silently slicing glassy waters; tropicbirds swirling above their northernmost breeding colony. And—just once—the utterly humbling, transfixing experience of being escorted for several hours by a pod of orcas. Gazing eye to eye as they plunged sideways beneath us, their mouths large enough to swallow our stern, the males' dorsal fins projecting above our heads. A sense of menace that transmuted, through shared moments at the surface of the sea, into communion.

Or watching, say, a flock of five hundred Western sandpipers on a Mexican mudflat, knowing they are about to lift into flight—as if a single organism, flashing white, dark, then light again, as they abruptly shift directions—and then wing their bodies, smaller than my fist, to tundra flats north of the Bering Straits.

And these hummingbirds in front of my eyes, signaling with the full force of their fierce, dense energies, that life is not to be lived partway. That every single moment must be a blur of feathers, a deep suck of nectar.

Natural history renews us as it scrubs clean our vision of the world. We need it to counter despair—there *is* durable beauty in this world. And we need it as an essential guidepost as we retrack our collective behavior toward more harmonious ways.

In the pages you hold, twenty-two voices—women and men, poets and scientists, musicians and teachers—declare how paying attention has changed their lives, and how it can change the world. You'll hear how attentiveness to inner/outer nature has made their lives less boring and more fun. How it has made them better thinkers, better neighbors, more fully alive. How it has encouraged humility and insight, protected their sanity and even their lives.

Enjoy their stories. Celebrate this bountiful beauty. Then step outside. What will you witness, this next moment?

Crazy about Nature

Like Thoreau, I wish to speak a word for nature, for natural history and the amateur tradition in particular. An amateur is led by the nose, or by the spirit, toward and into something that he or she comes to love. It is not a matter of schooling, or professional advancement or the usual rewards of the world. It is not about discipline or method—indeed, there may be a bit of madness in it, something that violates common sense and the admonitions of the rational mind. Why spend all that time, why clutter your brain with so much useless knowledge, why digress so emphatically from the proven and necessary pathways that lead to success with honor? The amateur turns from such questions with a smile. There is no point arguing. One's taste in life, as in food, cannot be disputed. The amateur loves whatever feeds the spirit.

Before there was biology, ecology, the National Science Foundation, there was natural history. Its culture heroes were all amateurs, self-taught mavericks and explorers. Think of Gilbert White, inventor of "parochial history," or his disciple Thoreau, who discovered forest succession while reporting to "a journal of no very wide circulation." Think of Darwin idling through the university, drinking, hunting, and gambling, flunking first medicine and then law before eventually graduating in divinity while taking elective after elective in botany and geology. When Captain Fitzroy came looking for a naturalist to take on board the *Beagle*, Professor Henslow realized that all his other students had secured positions in their chosen careers; none were available but the feckless Darwin, who eagerly signed on. Think of John Muir, who excelled at mechanical engineering and was offered a partnership after automating the carriage factory where he worked. Had it not been for the accident that left him temporarily blind, we would not have his thousand-mile walk to the gulf, his love affair with Yosemite, or the Sierra Club, not to mention volumes of first-rate nature writing. All of these people were largely self-taught, contrarian in their sensibilities, and more at home in the field than in the library. Their example prompts me to ask how natural history comes to feed the spirit, lighten the heart, and enhance the overall quality of life.

The journey began, for me, on the asphalt pavements and concrete sidewalks of urban New Jersey, where nature was dismally circumscribed by commerce and industry. I grew up there, yearning for the clean water, green woods, and blue skies of rural Connecticut, where we had a family cottage. Each summer I would hear stories about my grandfather, the minister, who had built the cottage and collected butterflies. It was fun to pore over the big old guidebooks with marginal notes in his slender, clerical hand; they reflected a time when the cottage sat in the middle of a meadow, surrounded by wildflowers, before the forest had begun to grow up after World War II. Nearby were other guidebooks to insects, ponds, and minerals; I used to spend hours copying down mysterious, esoteric names—*ana-*

baena, xanthosiderite, basidiomycetes–loving the sound and secrecy of the words, as if they rendered all nature somehow knowable and familiar. It was one way to escape the depressing prospect of winter in the city, with its school and church and blighted landscapes. The lake seemed such a rich and powerful place, so remote and exotic to an urban kid. Each trip felt like passing through the looking glass into a dream world where anything could happen.

But it was high school biology that turned me toward natural history in a serious way. This was in 1961, before the molecular wars and genetic engineering, and bio still meant dissections, microscopes, drawings on the blackboard, and forced marches through the phyla. Mr. Robertshaw, not long out of college, wore the requisite Cold War suit of navy blue and wing-tip shoes that belied his intense feeling for the organism. His course deepened and illuminated my experiences of nature at the lake. It pro-vided a vocabulary and a framework that would organize and relate them to one another. It also provided tools for observing, collecting, and classifying: insect nets, spreading boards, illus-trated keys, forceps, and collecting bottles, plus microscopes, with all their attendant apparatus of slides, stains, eyedroppers, and cover glasses. Thus armed, I began an earnest inventory of all the rocks, minerals, insects, fish, and plants around the lake. Now I knew how to look and what to look for.

Like the early explorers, I felt surrounded by unaccountable wonders and riches. Cigar box after cigar box soon filled with mounted insects cataloged by order (Hymenoptera, Odonata). A big glass jar of pig's feet from the deli held a lump of swamp muck that burst into life when I added water; it was marvelous to observe this miniature in vitro community morph through ecological succession. I loved drawing the transparent organ-isms that cruised and tumbled across the bright circular field of the microscope (*Euglena, Cyclops, Vorticella*). It felt like looking deep into nature through the eyes of God.

The physical world came next, through intro geology in college, where a young volcanologist described exciting discoveries along the Mid-Atlantic Ridge. He had worked in Iceland, scrambling over the newest, hottest rocks on the planet and dodging lava bombs during eruptions. Once, trapped on Surtsey, he had barely escaped with his life. It sounded impossibly romantic, much more dramatic than sectioning varved clays or measuring the strike and dip of beds. We learned how continental drift and the emerging theory of plate tectonics could explain places like Surtsey. Results from the International Geophysical Year were just coming in. One day the professor rushed into class waving a journal. "Paleomagnetism!" he shouted. "The IGY data proves we were right about plate tectonics!" The class burst into applause. Here we were, just college students but already standing on tiptoe at the frontiers of knowledge. Education could hardly get any better. And yet this was my last course in anything that could be called natural history.

Ironically, it took the U.S. Army to confirm my naturalist's avocation. Assigned to the Defense Language Institute in Monterey, California, I wandered the Big Sur coast on weekends, spending the evenings reading the poetry of Gary Snyder and Robinson Jeffers. It was not long before I discovered John Muir's and Clarence King's writings on the Sierra, which quickly became the dream destination for every free weekend or seasonal leave. Both Muir and King had exulted in the grand narrative of the range, written in the sublime language of uplift and glaciation, but Muir had also noticed the small things: a fly or a grasshopper on a granite dome, a water ouzel dipping and darting about a rushing stream. For him, everything was connected to everything else. I wanted to be like him, enjoying a hardy freedom in the open air, surrounded by exuberant wild things and magnificent landscapes, feeling at home everywhere. He was an adventurer, a writer, and a naturalist, self-taught, self-reliant, and living by his wits in the greatest place on earth. What could be better?

I began carrying a copy of Storer and Usinger's *Sierra Nevada Natural History*, which provided a comprehensive and ecologically organized guide to what I was seeing on the ground. It was an education between covers, a pocket manual to being John Muir. Here was the beginning of a lifelong practice of becoming native: learning to weave the stories in the land together with your own story—human, natural, and personal history all bound up together.

I came back from California and resumed grad school in literature convinced that nature writing ought to be studied and taught. No one was aware of what we now call "creative nonfiction" and "ecocriticism," and very few lit profs had ever thought of taking their students into the field, let alone into the wilderness, so that they could experience for themselves the power of place that had inspired writers like Jeffers and Muir. My literary friends were suspicious of science in any form and treated their own ignorance as a privilege, while my scientist friends thought nature writing had too much mushy subjectivity. Neither side seemed to recall that natural history had emerged as both field-based observational science and a literary genre—not a hybrid, but an original synthesis.

In an age enamored of exact science and poststructural semiotics, this primeval linkage was bound to arouse suspicion. To the scientists it removed the comforting, hygienic allure of numbers and formulas, which promise a kind of security. Observation, so crucial for naturalists and explorers, seems less reliable than controlled experiment. In science, as in the courts of law, eyewitness testimony can so easily be cast into doubt. And narrative, with its inherent bias of speaker and point of view, can be accused of distortion or subjectivity. On the other side, natural history's emphasis on direct observation, telling details, and objective reality resists the tendency to see everything as some sort of "text" that has been socially constructed and therefore has no essential meaning, or even being, apart from the "play of difference" among arbitrary signs.

Despite all the sound and fury of these debates, story remains both the oldest and the most pervasive technology that humans have devised for constructing, preserving and transmitting knowledge. And natural history is as much story as nature. That's why it connects so readily to the humanities, with their critical inquiry into values, images, or beliefs; to the arts, with their expressive powers; and to mythology and religion, with their sacred places, magical realism, and impulse to link moral and cosmological truth. The literature of nature and exploration fascinated me because it drew deep truths from real experience. Charles Darwin's narrative of the *Beagle* voyage depicted a man coming into his vocation. John Muir's first summer in the Sierra was a story of conversion. Aldo Leopold's shack sketches revealed how he and his family had found, in restoring a worn-out farm, their meat from God. These teachers had all found in the practice of natural history both a calling and a mission. It centered them emotionally, intellectually, spiritually, and professionally. They exemplified, for me, the ideal of a whole and balanced life.

But realizing one's vocation and finding a position may only be mileposts along the way. Some are born wanderers, some choose to wander, and some have wandering thrust upon them, especially in academe. I was thrust first into Utah and the Great Basin, then to the prairies of Minnesota, and eventually into the

Ohio Valley. It was easy at first, leaping upon the mountains or exploring the desert mazes where Anasazi had dwelt, glorying in the epic story of geologic time just as I had in the Sierra. But moving to Minnesota proved a much greater challenge. There was not much poetry or nature writing to guide me, and for a lover of mountains, the prairie held little scenic appeal. Look toward the horizon, and all you might see would be a solitary bur oak, a silo, or a feed mixer that looked like some kind of lunar module.

It took several cycles of seasonal change to reveal the land-scape's hidden dimensions: innumerable spring wildflowers blooming from winter-bleached grass, or immense rivers of migrating birds that filled every shallow depression in April fields with hungry song. You had to stay put to notice things like that. You had to enlarge your sense of place to include both time and distance, as well as biota that moved across continents. Where was home to a migrating goose? I might have a wintry image of Minnesota, all ice crystal and northern lights, but the goose would see it only as sweet, soft mud, waste corn, and a million tiny ponds scattered like rose petals along its flight path to Manitoba. These ancient, recurring cycles defined the char-acter of the landscape as indelibly as its low-relief hummocky terrain. The prairie was truly a fusion of geological and biologi-cal time. I began to wonder if migration might offer a paradigm for coping with the rootlessness of professional life.

Meanwhile, up north the Boundary Waters offered another kind of natural history lesson. Canoeing through the mazes of lakes proved more intimate, intricate, and challenging than hiking in the mountains. There, if you got lost or disoriented, you could always navigate by streams, landforms, and elevation, eventually making your way out to a road. But the Boundary Waters had no commanding summits, drainages, or other obvious landmarks, and you could not walk out across country. Without a map, you'd be utterly lost. Travel by canoe meant being immersed in the land, nose to nose with its plants and creatures; you were embedded, absorbed, with no aesthetic distance. The landscape was as much felt, heard, or smelled as seen. It was difficult to capture on film. The scenery was not self-composing, as in the mountains, and you had to resort to visual circumlocution to evoke some of the most characteristic features, such as the whine of mosquitoes or the taste of blueberries.

In the Boundary Waters I learned natural history mainly from rangers and scientists who worked directly in the field. They had learned how much of the place's character depended on what could not be seen with the naked eye, either because it was a matter of ecological relationships, food webs and the like, or because it involved processes that transpired across a time frame that exceeded a person's memory.

Ecologists had realized the crucial role of fire in the Boundary Waters, where "dry lightning" will ignite a given area once every hundred years under average conditions. Since that period is longer than a human life, you can't "see" the fire cycle, but every species that lives in these northern forests must adapt to its curve. Hence, white cedars grow along lakeshores; white and red pines grow tall and lay on thick insulating bark; aspens send up clones from underground roots; and jack pines, which need bare soil to sprout, keep their cones sealed up until a fire comes through and burns them open, releasing tiny winged seeds. Each of these adaptations can easily be observed, but to link them together with the fire cycle requires an act of imagination, a facility of "seeing the unseen." To study the Boundary Waters from the bow of a canoe was not only to cultivate the virtues of intimacy, patience, and attentiveness, but also to learn the importance of intangible and invisible things. So much of the quality of our lives depends on relationships, which can't be weighed, measured, quantified, or even directly observed. We use stories to make them visible.

By now, my own story was becoming clearer and clearer, at least with respect to natural history. The next move took the family to Cincinnati, where, amazingly, I found more wildness and profusion of life than ever before. Admittedly, Cincinnati, and the Rust Belt in general, were never high on my list. What did they have to offer a wilderness guy? Plus, the move was professionally traumatic: I had lost my bid for tenure and gone over to the dark side by accepting a deanship at a university for adult learners. What's more, I had just gotten married and we had a baby on the way. Life comes at you fast. But, as I learned, it also comes *to* you. Moving to the city, which had always seemed incompatible with nature and wilderness, actually opened a whole new realm of natural history.

The Zen master Shunryu Suzuki wrote, "In the beginner's mind there are many possibilities; in the expert's mind there are few." Becoming a parent gives you intense, invaluable training in beginner's mind. I'm not talking just about labor, diapers, and sleepless nights, although these do factor in. I'm talking about waking up to the world. For young kids, everything is new and vivid, glowing with mystery. To step out the front door is to land on an unknown continent. If you want to keep up with them, you have to slow down. Being smaller, they are closer to the earth, and they notice *everything*: the dove feather caught in a sidewalk crack, the gumball pecked by warblers, the bird's-nest fungi, small as peas, growing in the mulch at the foot of a Norway spruce. Once attuned to the near-at-hand, I noticed more colorful distractions: the twenty-four species of birds that showed up within two blocks of our house, the fireflies rising

into the treetops on hot July nights, the deer and possums sauntering through, nibbling jewelweed and hostas. For a wilderness
expert, these encounters with urban nature were both exhila-
rating and troubling. I had never imagined that there was so
much going on, nor how much it would force me to rethink
cherished environmental ideas.

When you stay in one place, you begin to notice patterns and
processes, such as ecological succession; you start thinking of
wilderness in terms of time instead of space. You begin to sense
how the place where you are is connected to larger dimensions
and arrays, such as the bioregion, the continent, or even the
biosphere itself. All this leads to a more complex and expansive
sense of ecological identity and a practice of natural history that
is at once more personal and more nuanced. For example, the
Cincinnati biota manifests a diverse array of alien and native
species, which have begun to co-adapt in interesting ways. Take
the Amur honeysuckle, a notorious invasive imported to stabi-
lize road cuts and reclaimed strip mines. It loves our degraded,
calcareous soils and unstable hillsides but also woody edges,
where it chokes out native shrubs, wildflowers, and saplings.
Much sound and fury, along with buckets of sweat, are spent
trying to extirpate it from our parks, to little avail. Yet now I
hear from a biologist friend that at his university, where the
playing fields are all edged with honeysuckle, the woodcock
have been nesting in the thickets and coming out at dawn to
do their sky dance before the players stagger out of bed. This
arrangement of native and alien species seems to be working,
at least for the woodcock, who benefit from the humans who
disturbed the land to create both the grassy clearing and the
edge that favors the honeysuckle that creates thickets perfect
for sheltering their nests.

Now, after twenty years, I still live in Cincinnati and practice natural history as both a sojourner and a traveler, exploring the neighborhood and visiting more remote and exotic places, some new, and some familiar from past trips. Everything knits together and converges. There are even times when I feel the exhilaration of a Humboldt or a Darwin, realizing how distant places are connected by similar processes or stories. Tennyson's Ulysses declared, "I am a part of all that I have met," but the reverse seems equally true: Every place I have lived has become a part of me. Practicing natural history, even as an amateur, has deepened all those connections. It helps one become native to a place, so that wherever you are set down, there you can orient yourself and begin to live. It is comforting, too, to discover familiar organisms in distant places, like John Muir finding a water ouzel in the icy fastnesses of Glacier Bay, when he was cold and hungry and down on his luck. Maybe this is why I always wander around the edges of motels or rest areas, checking the weeds and flowers. It helps to take your bearings. And in time, you realize that every place you have lived and worked is one of your homes and that you can always go back, circling like a migratory bird. In this way, home begins to feel less like the Ohio Valley, the Great Basin, or the Boundary Waters, and more like the continent itself, North America, Turtle Island.

Time washes over, under, around, and through a place like this, not just at personal or ecological scales, but also with geological grandeur. Walk down any Cincinnati ravine and you will find slabs of upturned Ordovician limestone knobby with fossil brachiopods (*Rafinesquina, Herbertella*); this land was their land a mere 450 million years ago. Or take the Ohio River, a very young stream whose present course more or less follows the front of the Pleistocene ice sheets that pushed down from Canada, damming the streams flowing north from the Kentucky mountains. Notice, too, how the river's arc also follows the contoured edge of the climate zone, which in turn follows the average path of the jet stream. Twelve thousand years ago, there were no alien species in Cincinnati, and no native species either, because the land was covered by six hundred feet of ice. If you live in one place and pay attention, a sense of deep time begins to form.

Both continental citizenship and a deep sense of the past are necessary, I believe, for a sustainable civilization. Imagining a deep past makes it possible to imagine a deep future, which is the ground of hope. Even in the damaged and degraded landscapes where most of us live, in old Rust Belt cities like mine, we can see healing processes at work, the woods undergoing succession, the animals starting to return. Paying attention to these processes is indeed precious, for it lightens our hearts and opens our minds. Knowledge is value; the more we understand the living world around us, the more curiosity and delight we experience, and the more alive we feel. "Nature deficit disorder" is not just for kids; it can afflict us at any age. Two million years of evolution have exquisitely tuned us to respond to the living world, upon which our ancestors had to depend for everything. Biophilia may be no more than a survival adaptation, but how forcefully it compels us. Just watch how your kids react whenever they spy an animal.

I love natural history because it helps me live in the present. It's good for society because it fosters sustainability, it's good for kids because it connects them to place and opens their eyes; it's good for me because it helps me become native in a nomadic professional life. The sense of wonder is as liberating as it was for Coleridge's Ancient Mariner, who forgot his misery when he looked at beautiful sea creatures and was suddenly able to pray.

The albatross fell from his neck. In the end natural history is good for the soul. It gives me delight and makes me feel at home. And it makes me want to share the gifts, sometimes even to the point of tedium. I can't forget my daughter taking aside a friend who had come over to play. "Be careful," she warned. "My dad is crazy about nature!"

Noctambulism

Late last March, snow settled unexpectedly across England, taking the country by surprise. Spring had arrived a week previously: Black buds had popped green on the ash trees. But then the winds swung round to northerly, the temperature sank, and winter made its comeback. Trucks moved patiently over the roads, whirring out fans of salt and stone. Children created an ice-slide on a quiet road near my house, and queued up in jostling lines, polishing the ice to the consistency of milk-bottle glass. A friend wrote from his home in Hope Valley in the Peak District to say he had spent two days out tracking Arctic hares there. He spoke of big beluga drifts of snow, and of the hares, still in their white fur, moving unhurriedly between them.

The story of the hares set me thinking, and the falling snow set me dreaming, as it always does. I decided that I would travel up to the Lake District, and go for a long night-walk in the Cumbrian mountains. Winter is the best time to night-walk, you see, because snow perpetuates the effect of moonlight, which means that on a clear night, in winter hills, you can see for a distance of up to thirty miles or so. I know this because I have seen that far several times before. Several, but not many, because in order to go night-walking in winter mountains, you require the following rare combination of circumstances: a full moon, a hard frost, a clear sky, and a willingness to get frozen to your core.

Night-walking—a.k.a. noctambulism. Noctambulism is usually taken to mean sleepwalking. But this is inaccurate: It smudges the word into somnambulism. Noctambulism means walking at night, and you are therefore etymologically permitted to do it asleep or awake. Generally, people noctambulize because they are in search of melancholy, or rather a particular type of imaginative melancholy. Franz Kafka wrote of feeling like a ghost among men—"weightless, boneless, bodiless"—when he walked at night.

I have found another reason for being out at night, however, and that is the wildness which the dark confers on even a mundane landscape. Sailors speak of the uncanny beauty of seeing a well-known country from the sea, the way that such a perspective can make the homeliest coastline seem strange. Something similar happens to a landscape in darkness. Coleridge once compared walking at night in his part of the Lake District to a newly blind man feeling the face of a child: the same loving attention, the same deduction by form and shape, the same familiar unfamiliarity. At night, new orders of connection assert themselves: sonic, olfactory, tactile. The sensorium is transformed. Associations swarm out of the darkness. You become even more aware of landscape as a medley of effects, a mingling of geology, memory, movement, life. New kinds of attention are demanded of you, as walker, as human. The landforms remain, but they exist as presences: inferred, less substantial, more powerful. You inhabit a new topology. Out at night, you understand that wildness is not only a permanent property of land—that it is also a quality that can settle on a place with a snowfall, or with the close of day.

Over the past two centuries in particular, however, we have learned how to deplete darkness. *Homo sapiens* evolved as a diurnal species, adapted to excel in sunlit conditions, and ill-equipped to maneuver at night. For this reason, among others, we have developed elaborate ways of lighting our lives, of neutralizing the claims of darkness upon us, and of thwarting the circadian rhythm. The extent of artificial lighting in the modernized regions of the Earth is now so great that it produces a super-flux of illumination easily visible from space. This light, inefficiently directed, escapes upward before being scattered by small particles in the air—such as water droplets and dust—into a generalized photonic haze known as sky glow. If you look at a satellite image of Europe taken on a cloudless night, you will see a lustrous continent. Italy is a sequined boot. Spain is trimmed with coastal light, and its interior sparkles like a rink. Britain burns brightest of all. The only significant areas of unlit land are at the desert margins of the continent: the northern stretches of the Sahara, and the ruined terrain around the Aral Sea, where water has surrendered to sand.

The stars cannot compete with this terrestrial glare and are often invisible, even on cloudless nights. Cities exist in a permanent sodium twilight. Towns stain their skies orange. The release of this light also disrupts long-established natural rhythms. Migrating birds collide with illuminated buildings, thinking them to be daytime sky. The leaf-fall and flowering patterns of trees—reflexes that are controlled by perceptions of day length—are disrupted. Glowworm numbers are declining because their pilot lights, the means by which they attract mates, are no longer bright enough to be visible at night.

By the time I reached the mountains, it was late afternoon. The snow line was regular at a thousand feet, dividing the world into gray and white, lower and upper. It was clear from the mood of the sky that another big fall was coming. Dark clouds had started to hood the Earth from the east, and the brown burnt light of imminent snow was tinting the air. Scatters of thin sleet were falling. My cheeks and nose fizzed with the cold.

The path to the upper ground switchbacked from the lake-shore through tall oak woods. Old coarse snow lay in rows between the trees, and in rings around their bases. Where I brushed against branches and leaves, snow spilled onto me like sugar. I met three other people, all of whom were descending. On each occasion we spoke briefly, acknowledged the extraordi-nariness of the land in this weather, and went our ways.

After half an hour, I reached the wide corrie that holds Bleaberry Tarn, and behind which rises the line of peaks that includes Red Pike, High Stile, and High Crag. Looking to my east and north, all I could see were white mountains. Distant snowfields, on mountains whose names I did not know, gave off bright concussions of late light. The wind was cold, and blowing into me. It was already so strong that I had to lean into it at a five-degree vaudeville tilt.

By the time I got to the ridge, at over two thousand feet, the snow had thickened to a blizzard. Visibility was no more than a few meters. The white land had folded into the white sky, and it was becoming hard even to stand up in the wind. I would need to find somewhere to sleep out the worst of the storm, so I cast about for sheltered flat ground, but could see none.

Then I came across a tiny tarn, roughly circular in shape, perhaps ten yards in diameter, pooled between two small crags, and seemingly frozen solid. The tarn ice was the milky gray-white color of cataracts, and rough and dented in texture. I pad-ded out to its center, and jumped gently a couple of times. It did not creak. I wondered where the fish were. The tarn was, if not a good place to wait out the storm, at least the best place on offer. It was flat, and the two crags gave some shelter from the wind. My sleeping bag and bivouac bag would keep me warm enough. And I liked the thought of sleeping there on the ice: It would be like falling asleep on a silver shield, or a lens. I hoped that when I woke, the weather would have cleared enough for some night-walking.

The blizzard blew for two hours. I lay low, got cold, watched the red reeds that poked up from the ice flicker in the wind. Hail fell in different shapes, first like pills, then in a long shower of rugged spheres, the size of peppercorns. Over half an hour, the hail turned to snow, which had the texture of salt and fell hissing onto the ice. I had begun to feel cold, deep down, as though ice were forming inside me, floes of it cruising my core, pressure ridges riding up through my arms and legs, white sheaths forming around my bones.

I must have slept, though, for some hours later I woke to find that the snow had stopped and the cloud cover had thinned away, and a late-winter moon was visible above the mountains: just a little off full, with a hangnail missing on the right side, and stars swarming round it. I got up, and did a little dance on the tarn, partly to get warm, and partly because if I looked backward over my shoulder while I danced, I could see my moon-shadow jigging with me on the snow.

I had woken into a metal world. The smooth unflawed slopes of snow on the mountains across the valley were iron. The deeper moon-shadows had a tinge of steel blue. Otherwise, there was no true color. Everything was grays, black, sharp silver-white. Tilted sheets of ice on the ridge gleamed like tin in the moonlight. The hailstones lay about like shot or ball bearings, millions of them, grouped up against each rock and nested in snow-hollows. The air smelled of minerals and frost. Where

I had been lying on the tarn, the ice had melted, so that there was a shallow indent, shaped like a sarcophagus, shadowed out by the moonlight.

To the south, the mountain ridge curved gently round for two miles. It was as narrow as a pavement at times, at others as wide as a road, with three craggy butte summits in its course. To the east and west, the steep-sided valleys, unreachable by the moonlight, were in such deep black shadow that the mountains seemed footless in the world.

I began walking the ridge. The windless cold burned the edges of my face. These were the only sounds I could hear: the swish of my breathing, the crunch my foot made when it broke through a crust of hard snow, and the woodlike groans of ice sinking as I stepped down on it. I passed an ice dune that was as smooth and glassy as the sill of a weir. My shadow fell for yards behind me. Once, stopping on a crag-top, I watched two stars fall in near-parallel down the long black slope of the sky.

When I came to a big frozen pool of water, I took a sharp stone and cut a cone-shaped hole in the white ice where it seemed thinnest. Dark water glugged up into the hole, and I knelt and dipped my mouth to the ice, and drank. I caught up a handful of snow, and patted and shaped it in my hands as I walked, so that it shrank and hardened into a little white stone of ice.

Where the ground steepened, I moved from rock to rock to gain purchase. On the thinner sections I walked out to the east so I could look along the cornice line, which was fine and delicate and proceeded in a supple curve along the ridge-edge and over the moon trench, as if it had been engineered.

Several small clouds drifted through the sky. When one of them passed before the moon, the world's filter changed. First my hands were silver and the ground was black. Then my hands were black and the ground silver. So we switched, as I walked, from negative to positive to negative, as the clouds passed before the moon.

To be out by night in a forest, by a river, on a moor, in a field, or even in a city garden is to know it differently. Color seems absent, and you are obliged to judge distance and appearance by shade and tone: Night sight requires an attentiveness and a care of address undemanded by sunlight.

And attention—care of address—is a moral refocusing as well as a physical one. The novelist Iris Murdoch knew this. She wrote repeatedly and brilliantly about the idea of "attention," a concept on which she based her moral philosophy. "Attention," Murdoch proposed, is an especially vigilant kind of "looking." When we exercise a care of attention toward a person, we note their gestures, their tones of voice, their facial expressions, their turns of phrase and thought. In this way, by interpreting these signs, we proceed an important distance toward understanding the hopes, wishes, and needs of that person. This "attention," Murdoch noted, is the most basic and indispensable form of moral work. It is "effortful," but its rewards are immense; for this attention, she memorably wrote, "teaches us how real things can be looked at and loved without being seized and used, without being appropriated into the greedy organism of the self."

This ideal of "attention," of a compelling particularity of vision, obtains to landscapes as well as to people. It is harder to dispose of anything, or to act selfishly toward it, once one has paid attention to its details. This is an environmentalist's truth, as well as a humanist's. It's for this reason that the most inspiring travelers through wild landscapes—from Samuel Taylor Coleridge to Barry Lopez—have been attentive, in the sense that Iris Murdoch and Simone Weil meant that word, to the terrains through which they have moved. Their imaginations have

responded with gripping exactitude to certain forms of matter (ice, rock, light, sand, moorland, water, air), and to certain
arrangements of space (altitude, edges, valleys, ridges, plains,
horizons, slopes). Comically, earnestly, lyrically, ecstatically,
anecdotally, or beautifully, these travelers have approached
their chosen landscapes with an eye to their uniqueness. In so
doing, they have primed a space within which those landscapes
can be respected—can come to seem less seizable and usable by
the greedy human self.

Out walking at night, you become of necessity super-atten-
tive: keenly aware of yourself and your passage through place.
But you also find yourself abolished, pummeled exhilaratingly
into insignificance by the spaces that surround you. The astonishment of the night-walker has to do with the unconverted and
limitless nature of the night sky, which in clear weather is given
a depth by the stars that far exceeds the depth given to the diurnal sky by clouds. On a cloudless night, looking upward, you
can experience a sudden flipped vertigo, the sensation that your
feet might latch off from the Earth and that you might plummet upward into space. Stargazing gives us access to orders of
events, and scales of time and space, that are beyond our capacity to imagine: It is unsurprising that dreams of humility and
reverence have been directed toward the moon and the stars for
as long as human culture has recorded itself.

Our disenchantment of the night through artificial lighting
may appear, if it is noticed at all, as a regrettable but eventually trivial side effect of contemporary life. That winter hour,
though, up on the summit ridge with the stars falling plainly
far above, it seemed to me that our estrangement from the dark
might constitute a profound event for our self-perception. We
are, as a species, finding it increasingly hard to imagine that
we are part of something that is larger than our own capac-

ity. We have come to accept a heresy of aloofness, a humanist belief in human difference, and we suppress wherever possible the checks and balances on us—the reminders that the world is greater than us or that we are contained within it. On almost every front, we have begun a turning away from a felt relationship with the natural world.

The blinding of the stars is only one aspect of this retreat from the real. On many fronts, there has been a prizing away of life from place, an abstraction of experience into different kinds of touchlessness. We experience, as no historical period has before, disembodiment and dematerialization. The almost infinite connectivity of the technological world, for all the benefits that it has brought, has exacted a toll in the coin of contact. We have in many ways forgotten what the world feels like. And as we have done so, many new maladies of the soul have emerged, unhappinesses that are complicated products of the distance we have set between ourselves and the world. We have come increasingly to forget that our minds are shaped by the bodily experience of being in the world—its spaces, textures, sounds, smells, and habits—as well as by genetic traits we inherit and ideologies we absorb. A constant and formidably defining exchange occurs between the physical forms of the world around us and the cast of our inner world of imagination. The feel of a hot dry wind on the face, the smell of distant rain carried as a scent-stream in the air, the touch of a bird's sharp foot on one's outstretched palm: Such encounters shape our beings and our imaginations in ways that are beyond analysis, but also beyond doubt. There is something uncomplicatedly true in the sensation of laying hands on sun-warmed rock, or watching a dense mutating flock of birds, or seeing snow fall irrefutably upon one's upturned palm.

The mountaineer Gaston Rebuffat identified a retreat from

the real as under way fifty years ago, in his memoir *Starlight and Storm*. And Rebuffat knew the real. He had spent his life in mountains by night and by day. He had bivouacked on north faces, in rock niches, in snow holes, and walked and climbed in all weathers and all hours. Starlight and storm, for Rebuffat, were indispensable energies, for they returned to those who moved through them a sense of the world's own forces and processes. "In this modern age, very little remains that is real," he wrote in 1956. "Night has been banished, so have the cold, the wind, and the stars. They have all been neutralized: the rhythm of life itself is obscured. Everything goes so fast, and makes so much noise, and men hurry by without heeding the grass by the roadside, its colour, its smell. . . . But what a strange encounter then is that between man and the high places of his planet! Up there he is surrounded by silence. If there is a slope of snow steep as a glass window, he climbs it, leaving behind him a strange trail."

After an hour's slow walking, I reached the flat-topped final summit of the ridge. Leading off it to the southeast was a steep little ice couloir, only twenty or thirty feet long, curved up at either edge, and sheeny with clear ice. It led down to a saddle and a small lower top. I sat down and heeled my way to the rim of the couloir, then luged down it, using my feet as brakes, striking ice chips with them, and feeling the cold black air crack against my face as I slid, so that it seemed as though I were passing through shattering plates of ice, until I slowed to a halt. Then I cleared some space among the rocks of the outcrop, pitched my tiny tent, and tried to sleep.

Sleep was almost impossible; the cold was so great, and the ground so uncomfortable. Before sunrise I got up, stretched, stamped my feet, and blew into my cupped hands. Then I walked over to the hard drifts of snow on the eastern side of the outcrop and cut a snow-seat, in which I sat and watched as dawn, polar and silent, broke over the white mountains.

The first sign was a pale blue band, like a strip of fine steel, tight across the eastern horizon. The band began to glow a dull orange. As the light came, a new country shaped itself out of the darkness. The hills stood clear. Webs of long, wisped cirrus clouds, in a loose cross-hatched network, became visible in the sky. Then the sun rose, elliptical at first, and red. I sat and watched that dawn, looking out over a country that was and was not England, with the cold creeping into me, and the white mountains receding into the white sky.

About half an hour later, the sky was a steady tall blue. I stood up, feeling the stiffness of the cold deep inside the joints of my legs, but also the early sunlight warm on my cheeks and fingers, and started to descend the mountain. As I got lower, the land began to free itself from the cold. Wafers of ice snapped underfoot. I could hear meltwater chuckling beneath the hard snow billows. Here and there, yellow tussocks of grass showed through the white. I was walking down out of winter.

Spilling from a black rock wall, I found a waterfall that was only partially frozen: a hard portcullis of ice, beautifully mottled by dark figures of thaw, and water falling behind it and from it. The water's turbulence was surprising and swift after the night-world. I stood for a while watching it, then drank from the stone cistern it had carved out beneath it, and snapped off an icicle to eat as I walked. Near my ledge, I found a gourd-shaped hole in a rock, in which water had gathered and frozen. I pried at the edges of the ice, and found I could lift out the top two inches of ice, revealing clear water beneath. The ice was as thick as the glass of a submarine's window, and I held it to my eyes, and briefly watched the blurred world through it. Then

I drank the sweet cold water beneath it and set off down the mountain, picking my path through the steep uneven ground, toward the fog.

The shoreline forest, as I came back through it, was busy with birdsong. I felt tired, but did not want to sleep. Near the head of the lake, just downstream of a small stone-and-timber bridge, where the river widened, there was a deep pool, glassy and clear, banked by grass.

I sat on the grass for a while and watched light crimp on the water's surface and flex on the stones that cobbled the stream-bed. I lay flat on the bank, rolled up my sleeve, and reached down to the bottom of the stream, where the water was weaving and unweaving the light, and picked a white stone, hooped once round with blue. I sat on the bank, holding the stone, and tried to list to myself the motions that were at that moment acting upon it: the Earth's 700-miles-per-hour spin around its axis, its 67,000-miles-per-hour orbit about the sun, its slow precessional straightening tilt within inertial space, and, containing all of that, the galaxy's own inestimable movement outward in the deep night of space. I tried to imagine into the stone, as well, the continuous barrage of photons—star photons and moon photons and sun photons—those spinning massless particles that were arriving upon the stone in their trillions, hitting it at 186,000 miles per second, as they were hitting me, and even with the stone still solid in my hand, I felt briefly passed through, made more of gaps than of joins.

I took off my clothes and waded into the water. It felt like cold iron rings were being slid up my legs. Dipping down, I sat in the water up to my neck, huffing to myself with the cold. The current pushed gently at my back. I listened to the whistles and calls of a farmer and saw sheep streaming like snow across the tilted green fields on the lake's far shore. In an eddy pool a few yards downstream, between two dark boulders, the curved rims of sunken plates of ice showed themselves above the surface. The sun was now full in the eastern sky, and in the west was the ghost of the moon, so that they lay opposed to each other above the white mountains: the sun burning orange, the moon its cold copy.

Perceiving a World of Relations

Stand at the edge of the marsh and listen to the
choral uproar of the frogs . . . surrender to their
shouting and allow yourself, too, like those pine
needles and that deer hair, to be refashioned
into the shape and the pattern and the rhythm
of the land.

—RICK BASS

I started picking up trash on the coast of Maine in the spring of
1993. It was the year my mother died, leaving a beach house to
the care of my sisters and me. Picking up garbage in a place she
loved was good for my grief.

On a warm afternoon in early May, I paddled into the
Sprague River marsh to collect garbage that had floated in over
the winter. There wasn't much. The stern hatch was far from
full that first spring.

Picking garbage out of the marsh became an annual spring
ritual. I recorded my collection over the first four or five years,
noting the increase and wondering where it came from. It didn't
take long to see that it was coming from beachgoers and fish-
ermen alike. Empty quarts of engine oil showed up in equal
measure to beach balls and plastic shovels.

Sixteen years later, I gather garbage during the fall and win-

ter, and just about every time I wander into the marsh I find endless pieces of plastic. Oil cans and oil jugs are less common, but
plastic bottles and bags are ubiquitous. It is too much to catalog.

I now know where all that tidal trash comes from. My mind
shifts to the streams and rivers I have come to know, the patterns of land use in this watershed, the flows of stormwater
through the estuary and the impact on all life downstream.
At the end of the line, I see plastic strewn in the wrack line,
wrapped up with seaweed and salt marsh hay.

The fact of my mind wandering through the watershed is
no coincidence. I've schooled myself on the imagery of water
and relatedness for years. My attention has been focused on
patterns, tides, lunar cycles, and what happens to water bodies
when it rains.

I'm a visual scientist by training. My focus on relatedness began
with the accumulating data indicating that attention has the
power to alter the way we process visual information—and hence
how and what we habitually see. With attention activated, so
went the argument, connections between simultaneously firing
neurons are strengthened. Those that become well connected
are like well-worn paths—easily accessed and easily traveled.
The neural paths themselves depend on where we have been
looking and whether we were truly attending.

After teaching ecopsychology for a decade, I wanted to see
more of the relatedness of the world. I was weary of our common
focus on objects, and the relentless pressure to buy more things.
I had come to the conclusion that our environmental crisis, the
fact of living in a world of loss, is ultimately a crisis of perception. I am now as certain as ever: Unless we commonly perceive
the interdependent reality within which we are all embedded,
we will never get ourselves out of the ecological mess we are in.

I began my practice by attending to contrast. I looked for edges and counted series of things like fence posts and windows. Soon these edges led my eye into patterns like ripples and leaves. Branching patterns began to bounce into view, so I looked for metaphors and evidence, like flocks of birds pointing to schools of fish, or forest composition revealing land use history. I studied phenomena like the "edge effect" and the movement of constellations across desert skies. I watched for the precise moment when the high tide began to ebb, signaling an otherwise invisible relationship between sun and moon.

Contrary to our Western notion that seeing is the obvious outcome of opening our eyes, this way of seeing is intentional and relational. In this case, the relationship is between the viewer and the viewed, but so too, the "thing seen" informs us of relatedness—of how things are similar, endlessly connected, and interdependent. In such a field of dense relations, receptivity—requiring our sincere engagement, as if opening long-clenched hands—is critical. For Goethe, seeing well required even more than being especially receptive. He began by "plunging into seeing." His practice included actively searching for patterns, qualities, and "exalted perceptual experiences." It was rigorous and curious. According to historian Theodore Roszak, "his eye for form and color was almost voluptuous; it caressed what it studied and felt its way in deep."

With the senses engaged like this, our attention is committed and cast outward. Colors become especially vibrant, and new forms jump into view, capturing still more of our attention. We forget ourselves, and habitual thoughts dissipate as if left behind in a fog. With my attention cast out over the salt marsh, I became spellbound by the daily high tide and fascinated by moving edges, by changing blues, greens, and light on water, and by the saturation of a wetland. As I watched the tides change over many monthly cycles, I began to sense great gravitational bodies tugging at one another. I, too, was tugged and began to feel slow pulses with the turning of the tides.

Having taught vision improvement in the 1980s, and having observed a significant number of people change their visual acuity by doing simple eye exercises, I was eager to try out this more qualitative form of practice with others. In the fall of 2001, a dozen students signed up for a course titled Ecological Perception and then followed me into the Arizona backcountry. Our intention was to immerse ourselves in natural landscapes for several weeks and to become skillful perceivers of patterns, metaphors, and the quality of our sensory relationships with the nonhuman world. Our first camp was in a ponderosa pine forest along Black Creek in the northeastern part of the state. The trees were one hundred and even two hundred feet tall, healthy and widely spaced, as in "presettlement" days. We did exercises designed to make ourselves especially good sensory receivers, to sharpen our acuity, improve our visual memory, and refine our depth perception. We studied animal tracks and stars, played visual games, and told stories about wandering among ponderosas. From my perspective, it was an experiment in perceptual practice. By the end of eight or nine days, I think it fair to say that all of us had altered our visual habits. No doubt, however, we all felt many more sensations in our reawakened bodies.

On the day of our departure from Black Creek, I became agitated for no apparent reason. I found myself hunched and crying by the creek, tears streaming. When asked why, I could not say. I became oddly irritated by the banter around camp as we took down tents and stuffed packs. Before hiking up the trail, I gathered everybody together, requesting that we walk in silence. I then started to cry again, saying something about learning to "love harder." Several hours later, we learned that the Twin Towers had been attacked that morning. It was 9/11.

We made a five-hour beeline back to the college, listening to the radio and looking for comfort. But when we regrouped the following day, after a night of television news, my students were agitated and frightened, and they insisted that we return to the woods. There was widespread drought at the time, and water in the nearby backcountry was very hard to find. Nonetheless, we hurried out of town, apparently all believing that we would be safer at the far northern end of the national forest.

We made camp during a sudden downpour, filling cooking pots with rainwater streaming off big blue tarps. But as if to save our lives, we resumed our practice. We did our daily exercises and, under the nightly instruction of my assistant, studied the stars with a kind of vengeance. By the last week, all of us had learned to recognize a large number of constellations. We learned their mythic stories as well, and most of us, I'm sure, were reminded of the Way of the Warrior each time Orion leaped into sight.

Back in the woods and under clear skies, we soon spoke of belonging in a wondrous universe, and some noted feeling at home as if for the first time. With my eye penetrating that wildly magnificent night sky, I wanted to throw myself into it—such was the sensation and ecstasy of feeling my place within a mysterious universe. Such was the immediacy of wonder.

Advertising and marketing budgets aimed at children topped $12 billion in 1997, spurring an increase in materialism and likely producing the record profits from teenage spenders in subsequent years. That same year Daniel Acuff, a child psychologist by training, published *What Kids Buy and Why: The Psychology of Marketing to Kids.* On this morning's business news, two of

Acuff's clients, Hasbro and Disney, announced a new partnership. The celebrated purpose of the partnership is to increase advertising of Hasbro toys through programming on expanded TV networks for children. The subtext of the news was that this will strengthen the economy; it will ensure a generation of well-trained consumers, their minds having been shaped to buy, their eyes so readily seduced.

Such highly conditioned consumerism is but one facet of modern consciousness. Suffice it to say that we are saturated by objectification and quantification. A certain sensibility arises when trained on hours, dollars, and things to buy. In part, it tends to be concerned with scores and rank and is thus competitive. It tends to be most interested in facts and being correct, and thus lacks imagination. I suspect that a yearning to throw one's self into the stars would be considered merely romantic, for such a sensibility also tends toward being detached and disembodied. According to David Kidner, author of *Nature and Psyche*, "The story of modern consciousness tells of the gradual separation of an increasingly self-conscious individual from its surroundings." He refers to this sorry condition as "the colonization of the psyche." It is why changing our minds, or, rather, changing the very stuff of our brains, is so critical.

Michael Merzenich, a neuroscientist, is the modern genius most responsible for discovering how "plastic" the brain is—or how dramatically the brain can change its structure and function. His findings regarding the age, speed, and degree of brain plasticity are radical. Neural restructuring can occur in both young and old; in blindfolded subjects, the visual cortex may be "remapped" to represent the sense of touch in a matter of days; and such restructuring now transforms speechless autistics into talkers. Modification in neural structure was front-page news in 1981, when the Nobel Prize in Physiology or Medicine went to neuroscientists David H. Hubel and Torsten Wiesel, but those findings were limited to relatively brief developmental periods in kittens. Merzenich's experiments have since shown that the age of the brain is not the limiting factor—it's the capacity to pay attention.

Merzenich claims that paying "close attention" is necessary for long-term plastic changes in the cortex. According to Merzenich, the nucleus basalis, the part of the brain that allows us to focus our attention, is "the modulatory control system of plasticity—the neuro-chemical system that, when turned on, puts the brain in an extremely plastic state." The difference between adult cats and kittens seen in earlier experimentation reflects the fact that a specific growth factor automatically turns on the nucleus for a specific "critical period," during which the brain is so plastic that its connectivity, or structure, can change with a single stimulus. In older brains, the nucleus basalis is activated only when something is personally "important or surprising, or if we make the effort to pay close attention." Without the growth factor automatically triggering the activation of the nucleus, paying attention requires work.

Paying attention changes the connectivity between neurons, altering neural networks and the function of our brains. What, then *is* attention? There are hundreds of definitions. Psychologist and cultural critic James Hillman claims that "attention means attending to, tending, a certain tender care of, as well as waiting, pausing, listening. It takes a span of time and a tension of patience." Paul Rezendes, an animal tracker, simply says, "Attention is care." A religious studies scholar, Huston Smith, beseeches us: "Wisdom! Attend!" Buddhists will say that true attention is when self-consciousness is replaced by awareness of the present, perhaps explaining why attention has been described as "rare and sacrificial."

Most fundamentally, attention is the capacity to join the contents of the mind and the "things" of the world. From a practical point of view, attention is a skill that requires effort. We get better at it if we practice. Ordinary, untrained attention "comes and goes without our consent," says Philip Novak, also a religious scholar. He claims that such ordinary attention is not something we do but something that happens to us. It is easily captured by what is bright, shiny, or appealing to the many shades of self-interest. But such untrained attention is also fickle and unreliable, stumbling through consciousness and the world alike.

Well-honed attention—as evidenced in trackers, mindfulness practitioners, athletes, hunters, artists, writers, ornithologists, and more—is something quite different. It can be focused narrowly or distributed across the entire visual field at will. Its focus can be internal (on the contents of mind) or external, and it can be sustained for long periods. It is penetrating, quick, and efficient, picking up signals that are altogether unseen by the untrained eye. In the lab, practiced attention translates into an increase in efficiency for detecting a target and accurately knowing what it is by 15 percent or more in every 200-millisecond eye fixation. Over a minute or two, such an increase in efficiency represents a great deal of additional visual information. According to Merzenich's way of thinking, a heightened capacity to attend also translates into a highly plastic—or highly adaptive—brain, changing continuously in response to incoming streams of information.

Psychologists have long been aware of the power of attention to enhance whatever we choose to look at. The finding that attention determines what we *will* see in the future, by way of altering neural structure now, is a more recent discovery. But as yet there has been little extrapolation about how shifting neural networks might also shift our perceptual tendencies.

What sort of sensibility might emerge with one's attention commonly cast out over a river? Could it be that a fluid, flexible form of consciousness—a certain sensibility—is born of attention to River? Could an internal ease arise after contemplating Lake's still depth? As children, might we learn the nature of transformation by watching tadpoles become frogs in the fecund months of spring? Might we then be predisposed toward a belief in our own potential to transform?

To our benefit, the world displays itself. The tide floods then ebbs, recedes and comes forth again—rhythmic, ceaseless, and reassuring like a well-spoken prayer; we might learn of faith. We see flow, meander, and seep in rivers and streams, informing our capacity for grace. On still nights we might see the moon reflected in ponds, lakes, and bays, and wonder at the Buddhist notion of "one, not two." Is there more than one moon, present in both water and sky? For a moment, we suspend our absolutes.

Let us imagine: Could it be that such a fluid consciousness may be critical to, say, negotiating water rights? Could we be both deeply informed by the organic wisdom displayed for us in a world beyond our own invention and still practical in the dense and demanding realm of environmental problem-solving? Could a deepened sense of stillness and a strengthened relational sensibility be particularly useful in our fragmented and nerve-racked world? To be more specific, could habits of attention be trained on the patterned world and inform our understanding of interdependence?

Patterns are elusive—they readily slip by our eye. In simple terms, they are likenesses gathered together, or repetitions in space. Diane Ackerman, author of *A Natural History of the Senses,* defines a pattern as an occurrence times three, and describes them as "visually succulent." Gregory Bateson, famous for his notion of "the pattern that connects," describes patterns as "the bones of the universe." Soetsu Yanagi, philosopher and art historian, claims that the value of patterns lies in their transformative powers, their "vitality and ability to metamorphose, symbolically, wisdom into its highest order." He adds that patterns "provide unlimited scope for the imagination."

With an eye tuned to patterns, similarity and associations—rather than distinctions or objects—become primary. The eye wanders in search of more likeness, more relatedness. "Things" get shifty and coalesce into new forms of logic. Sunflowers and pinecones become spirals, similar to the growth patterns of snail shells and the movement of water in whirlpools. So, too, spirals describe the hero's journey, metaphorically revealing the development of human consciousness. Familiarity with patterns in the visible world adds to our repertoire of recognition and leads the rational mind into imaginative and metamorphic modes, nudging us into deepened ways of knowing both the world and our own organic selves. With our attention focused on patterns, we soon see connectivity everywhere we look, with ourselves, the viewers, now woven into the fabric. We become less self-referenced, less interested in basic, causal relationships between ourselves and objects. This is antithetical to our Western, materialistic sensibility—so our attention is now further captured by novelty and surprise. We stretch to name the new patterns we see, and the world becomes more deeply known and richer. But perhaps because we cannot always name the gathering of likeness (is that a magnolia warbler, or a chestnut-sided warbler?); we wonder—and look again. It is an iterative process. We look, our attention captured, our neurons firing in response to the quest to name the pattern, the neural tracks laid down as we attend, the pattern becoming embedded in the brain and, as we say, more "familiar to the eye." The patterns we now look for become increasingly detailed. Seeking them intensifies our experience. We find ourselves saturated—our senses now so fully engaged, our bodies soon to follow. Pulsation, magnetism, and yearning are readily felt in response to incoming streams of information.

By developing the skill of attention, and by choosing to attend to patterns, we prepare ourselves to readily perceive relatedness and congruence. The world we perceive becomes more integrated and systemic in its nature, and more animated as it takes shape before our eyes. We naturally engage. We throw ourselves into the stars.

Sauntering toward Bethlehem

At the end of term one of my students came charging into my office full of excitement. "I've just been to *the* coolest seminar over at the genetics labs," he said. "They are going to produce a field-ready gene analyzer. Just imagine, you could get a chunk of bear dung, give it to the analyzer, and it will tell you what the bear was eating." I think he sensed my lack of excitement, because he stopped and asked what I thought. I said that it was very interesting, but wasn't there another way to find out what the bear was eating? He thought for a moment and said, "Oh, we could do stable isotope analysis and get trophic levels."

"Or?" I said.

"Well, I guess we could do some protein analysis and . . ." He could see he wasn't getting to me.

"Or?" I said. The conversation stopped.

"Well, what?" he asked.

"Well, we could watch the bear."

I have mixed emotions about this story. On the one hand, it captures a lot of what I worry about in science—the preference of technology over simplicity, the reification of particular forms of quantification over qualification, ultimately the separation of ecology from natural history. On the other, it also could be simply a matter of the passing generations: the grumpy old professor refusing to be impressed by the upstart youngster, a rude put-down to an attempt at a bridge between worlds. Maybe the story contains both. I suspect that a couple of hundred years ago there were grumpy old professors who were concerned about the effects those newfangled looking-glasses would have on their students' observations and understanding of their world, and students who were already dreaming of how to mount two telescopes on one frame to capture a magnified stereo image.

It is important to elaborate on the background to the conversation. At the heart of all my teaching is a belief in the importance of actually doing things, not just talking about them or seeing pictures of them or reading about what others have done. My student is doing just that—he is a lab assistant in a genetics project, performing work that is usually reserved for graduate students. He is actively engaged in research. The gene sequences that he works with are no less tangible—at least to him—for being invisible to the unaided senses. Why, then, my dissatisfaction?

At its base, I realize that what this story is about, what *my* story has been about, is a very simple love of wild things in wild lands and my attempt to encourage my students to think, even occasionally, in those terms. I am not nearly as interested in abstract questions as I ought to be. Twenty-five years ago one of my best teachers asked me, "What are you in this game for anyway?" and I replied, "I want to go to interesting places and see beautiful things." "Hmmph," she replied. "You won't get very far with *that* attitude."

She is probably right, but as Cormac McCarthy put it in

another context, "There is no such joy in the tavern as upon the road thereto." I have spent as much of my life as I can in interesting places and watching beautiful things, and if the results have been mostly qualitative and general I am willing to stand by them.

More and more I have come to believe that the context of any action may be at least as important as the action itself, and that this also applies to our learning and teaching. An analysis of bear dung that gives a precise distribution of foodstuffs consumed or fits the bear into some clearly defined trophic level doubtless has an elegance and beauty of its own, but it is neither the bear nor the berries that the bear ate, nor the crushed grass stems springing back from the bear's pugmarks, nor the taste of the morning air before anyone else in camp is awake, nor your feeling of breathless excitement that direct contact with the truly *other* can bring.

Realization of the differences between theory and practice came early. When I was still young enough to remember most things, my father took me to Ely Cathedral in England and showed me a great maze made in the colored stone slabs beneath the West Tower. He explained to me that this maze was based on medieval examples in France, where penitents would walk the maze on their knees over and over, with so many successful trips "counting" as a pilgrimage to the Holy Land. He then looked at me with a serious expression and said that he himself felt that the pilgrims would have "gotten a lot more out of an actual trip to the Holy Land."

The lesson stuck with me: You could learn certain things— and gain a measure of grace—by simulation, doing things that were *like* other things or *stood in* for other things. At the same time, however, something was always lost. It wasn't simply having the experience but missing the meaning. Rather, the experience itself *was* the meaning. One can earn Brownie points in heaven by following a maze, but think of all the experiences that one misses! I suspect that a medieval priest would say that those experiences are things of this world and that the whole point of pilgrimage is to get to another world, but think of all the opportunities for deeds good and bad that the pilgrim who takes the actual road will encounter! Both may arrive at the same destination in spirit, but they will not, cannot be the same in experience or understanding.

I am not sure just when I became a watcher of creatures. I know that my parents always encouraged my siblings and me to pay attention to plants and animals, but my earliest memory of "botanizing" is one of disappointment: being taken on what seemed a long walk in the dry California hills to see shooting stars, only to find that what we had come for were small plants, not blazing meteors. The generic name *Dodecatheon* stuck somehow—it had a magic all of its own, and hinted at a whole system of naming, and maybe then I started having a need for clarity in description, things being called what they were. There was no hint of the presence of a scientist or natural historian yet, but something happened with small flowers, long names, and a disappointed six-year-old that echoes down the years.

I grew up two blocks from a large regional park that abutted on protected watershed lands. Much of this land had been used for training during the Second World War, and then later as basing sites for anti-missile missiles. A quarter of a century of sun and wind and rain had done their work well, and in five minutes I could slip from the suburban 1960s into a romantic world of ruined barracks and silos, winding streams, California scrublands, and eucalyptus groves. I was lord of ten thousand acres that I seemed to share only with the red-tailed hawks and turkey vultures, stray cattle and occasional deer. At some point my interest in tracing the lines of the old military encampments gave way to a deeper interest in the plants and animals that had moved in behind the departing armies, or had never left in the first place. I wanted to know why vultures rocked, and whether hawks ate anything except snakes, and why lizards did "push-ups." Somehow the stories of the *non*-human landscape became more intriguing and mysterious than the stories of increasingly distant wars.

When I was thirteen, two tankers collided in the Golden Gate at the mouth of San Francisco Bay. Because it was winter, the bay was full of seabirds, waiting for warmer weather to return to the north. Almost at once thousands of oiled birds started washing up on shore. Most died before anything could be done for them, and much of what was done for the rest was done out of ignorance rather than knowledge, but it was a chance to see birds that were normally small black dots off the bow of a boat. I more or less moved in to the rehabilitation center, which was set up in a vast warehouse in the industrial section of town. At some point in the next three months someone came up with the idea of playing a recording of surf over the warehouse speaker system in order to make the birds "feel more at home." My favor-ite time was the late-night feeding, where we would step quietly from pen to pen, tubing murres and cormorants a mixture of vitamins and fish gruel, with the soft surge and sigh of the Pacific waves playing in endless loops above us.

I think my desire to mix science with natural history came from working with oiled birds over the next seven years. At the start nobody knew how to get the oil off feathers, much less what to do with a bird once it was cleaned. I learned to distrust authority, as when my ornithology professor solemnly told us that rhinoceros auklets eat plankton. My hand was up in an instant—"But they like herring." "How do you know?" "Well, I was just feeding one herring an hour before class." Practical experience beats theory and abstraction every time. Auklets will eat thawed herring, and so will pelicans, but a loon won't even look at a dead fish unless you "swim" it through the water toward it, and even then they much prefer live minnows.

In a word, my training was scattered. Like my future student I had the opportunity to see and touch and feel actual things, but my "laboratory" was mostly out of doors or with things big enough to see and hold unaided. As such, it was untidy, uncontrolled, and periodically either very wet or very hot and usually dirty. The most valuable thing this taught me was that the world itself was very messy, and much of the order that the scientific part of my training wanted was being imposed by the scientists, rather than being there to start with. Controlled experiments are all very well, but plants and animals have to deal with a lack of controls, and many combinations of organisms, traits, or behaviors just don't work very well. There are patterns and even harmonies, but there are also endless exceptions and discords, and I always seem to be drawn to the latter.

Much as I wish it were not so, I think a degree of loneliness and of being alone may be essential ingredients in the making of a naturalist. If this is so, then it raises some troubling questions about many of the well-meaning "environmental education" programs that have grown up since my childhood. Professional environmental educators seem to be caught between two contradictory poles. On the one hand, they are trying to instill certain "ecological principles" in their charges: ideas about connectivity, predators and prey, pollution, climate, watersheds, abstract ideas such as "ecosystems" and "succession." On the other, they are also trying to develop "group process," a degree of cohesiveness and inclusion in which each child is "task oriented" or at least not "running wild." Anyone who has spent much time trying to move around in the out-of-doors knows that one's likelihood of sneaking up on anything decreases with the size of the group trying to sneak. People together *will* talk, and what in one person's passage is an occasional snapping twig becomes noisy bushwhacking when repeated by many people.

Quite apart from the difficulty of keeping a group quiet enough for some good stalking, I suspect that the condition of being alone may lend itself to more serious and complete observation of one's surroundings. It is interesting to consider the different ways we tend to address language acquisition and appreciation of the "languages" of the nonhuman. In learning human languages it seems that everyone knows that there is nothing so good as complete immersion. You will pick up a new language much better if you are living in a situation where everyone else is speaking the "new" language as a matter of course. Having even one speaker of your native language with you reduces the effectiveness of learning enormously—it is *so* tempting to slip back into one's own familiar speech! By contrast, we encourage students to go into the wild in groups, thus limiting the possibility for true immersion in the languages of the Other.

Beyond increasing the likelihood that you will pick up subtle cues from the environment, a certain antipathy for the company of other humans may instill a greater desire for that of other creatures. People who spend much time wandering in the out-of-doors tend to have a degree of suspicion about laws, and the Law likewise has a suspicion about us. We are tramps, hiding behind hedges, leaping into or over ditches, coming home late in various states of disrepair. In his *Journal*, Thoreau speaks of how "Even in Virginia a naturalist who was seen crawling through a meadow catching frogs, etc., was seized and carried before the authorities."

A number of years ago I had a student who was very good

indeed in the out-of-doors. I chided him once for being late to a meeting, and he explained to me that he had been engaged in "car-ditching" on his way to school. I asked him what on earth he was talking about, and he explained that he had been trying to get to school without being seen, at least by humans. Every time he heard a car coming he would drop to all fours behind a bush, duck behind a tree, roll down an embankment. Doubtless this behavior would have looked extremely suspicious to any passing policeman, and downright strange to many of the rest of us, but I felt an immediate sense of kinship.

The natural historian is constantly confronted with the peculiarities of place or individual specimen. He or she is drawn to the exceptions, or, as one of my best teachers told me, we are attracted to the *variance*, not to the *mean*. Anyone who spends a good day in the field will soon realize that birds don't read textbooks. How many seemingly well-laid plans for a field season have been disrupted by the first few days' discoveries? I have a colleague who spent a quarter of a century studying one group of birds and coming up with a series of strong predictions that made beautiful sense within a theoretical framework. In the twenty-sixth year, everything changed. His only comment: "You need to know when to come home." There *are* general patterns, but they often break down on close examination, and in any case they are seldom so enticing as the delightful eccentricities of individual animals.

This sort of thinking doesn't sit well with a culture that expects scientists to be precise, quantitative, and best of all, definitive. Several years ago I tried to interest some public school teachers in a project involving the study of seabirds on an offshore island. The teachers were uniformly excited at the idea of their students "doing real research" and "working with scientists." Then they asked, "So, what will the students discover?" I replied, "I haven't a clue—this is original research." At that point the whole conversation dried up. People muttered about the importance of learning standards and the difficulty of developing rubrics under situations of uncertainty. One of the more forthright teachers said to me straight out that it was a matter of control: "You see, John, it is really important that the students don't get the sense that we don't know the answers."

Answers and questions come from many quarters. For someone who is convinced of the essential nature of actual experience I also find myself obsessed with books. Not the ever-more-popular "digital editions" but actual physical books. I think there is a common thread between the study of natural history and a passion for old books. There is something visceral about turning pages that have been turned countless times before, noting marginalia—from cryptic notes, to coffee stains and folded corners, to faint underlining that gives hints of previous readers—tracks in some strange new world of the mind. I cannot enter a house without looking for—and looking over—the bookshelves, the presence or absence of certain authors giving clues to personality, understanding, or focus.

Some of my favorite nonfiction reading has been accounts of travels and discoveries, especially if I have been to the places described, or have some hope of getting there. I am constantly on the lookout for things that I would have hoped to record had I been in that place at that time. When Champlain visited Maine's Frenchman Bay, on whose shores I am writing this essay, was his failure to record the presence of any birds in the seventeenth century evidence of absence or merely absence of evidence? I rejoice in the writers who share the details of their passage through a landscape and am disappointed by opportunities missed. After a long reluctance I have been drawn to Thoreau in large part by his inclusion of even the smallest elements of his surroundings in his writing. We read him and know when the first ice formed and the last ice melted 160 years ago. We can tell when the buds formed and when the leaves returned, and he draws us to our own observation.

Of all Thoreau's writing I still find *Walking* the most engaging. Thoreau seems to know that he is writing for the ages, and he does his best to paint a picture that is both immediate and real (the neighbor in the "Stygian fen") and abstract to the level of the sublime ("In wildness is the preservation of the world"). The title and central metaphor, however, are what really grab me. Thoreau is walking, and he wants us to walk with him. The entire essay is an invitation to get out, go do something, experience for yourself whatever may come around the corner, behind the hill. Early in the essay he engages in a bit of etymology, which one would like to be true, even if the professionals have ruled otherwise. Thoreau dwells on the verb "to saunter." He suggests that sauntering is a very particular *type* of walking that is essential to the true traveler and also has a touch of the divine: A saunterer, he suggests, is literally a *sante terre* on a journey to the Holy Land. It is here that I find the intersection of a small boy and his father in Ely Cathedral staring at a maze, and natural history, writing, and the value of experience.

Thoreau would have had little time for walking a maze as a surrogate for a true pilgrimage. He wants his reader out of doors, on the true highways and byways of the world, drinking in and recording everything that we see and feel, and organizing it in some sort of coherent scheme. The Holy Land that Thoreau is approaching is literally transcendental—he is dying—and also very real and present. The entire essay is filled with "everyday" imagery that most of us simply skip over. Thoreau thinks much of swamps and common wildflowers. He is less interested in the more or less predictable variety provided by human gardens; he wants the *wild*. He seems to suggest that at every turn we are at the edge of another and in some way grander world that is on the one hand subsisting quietly, unobserved, next to us but is constantly threatening to break through our conscious selves.

At the same time that Thoreau is encouraging us to be saunterers, to give up our attachments to place and the distractions of our everyday lives, he also cautions us against losing direction and purpose to a larger sense of mission. He reminds us that many so-called "saunterers" were little more than vagabonds and con-men who but pretended to be on pilgrimage. Merely ceasing to hurry from one human environment to the next is not sufficient to make one a true member of Thoreau's company; one must also in a sense be conscious of the passage we make, the things that we tend to pass over. I worry at times that I have allowed the metaphor of sauntering to cover up my own laziness or lack of engagement. I think that for all that the journey may be much better than the ultimate destination, there must *be* a destination or else it is too easy to slip from broad-minded observation to chaos.

Technology, planned experimentation, and an organized theoretical framework are important things if one is to do good science, but they are not the *only* things. In their voyage to the Sea of Cortez, Ed Ricketts and John Steinbeck said something to the effect that it is "important to know what one is doing." They also cautioned us against recording "one truth and many lies." Left to his own devices, I am sure, my student has the ability to learn *many* truths about a variety of organisms. As his teacher it is my job to help define a context for his questions, to remind him of what he is doing, and to ask, as gently as I can, whether what he is doing is worth the doing. I need to do this carefully. His questions may not be my questions, and the goal that he seeks may be very different from the ones that I have pursued.

The possibility of fruitful dialogue is not only there, however, but is of itself both an adventure and a journey.

In the long years since my own teacher cautioned me that I might not get very far with what I now see as an approach to a natural history, I have managed to circumnavigate the globe twice, I have seen many "beautiful things" in many "interesting places." I have seen Western grebes dance; I have seen shearwaters slide between Atlantic swells; I have walked Darwin's Sand Walk, and seen his frog in the marshes of Uruguay. I have come away with many more questions than answers, and at times I have found myself very alone. As I saunter on toward some Bethlehem of the mind, I feel that I am on a road with a whole ghostly company—Thoreau and Darwin, Steinbeck and Ricketts, my parents, and all the others who have chosen direct experience of the world over abstractions, who have limited patience with the indoors, and who have tried to take seriously the most important stricture in all of science: "Pay attention."

The Grounding of a Marine Biologist

Clouds of white dust billowed up and enveloped us. Before pulling my T-shirt over my head, I watched my brother turn into a white ghost as he struggled with his own shirt. We lay down on the brown bags of freshly made mesquite charcoal and breathed in the sharp odors of the charcoal mixed with the gritty dust of an old salt flat that the road plowed through. At last there were some sharp bounces and a grinding of gears as our father missed the downshift to get the old truck up and over a ridge and out of the dust. Eli looked up and grinned, always able to see the bright side of life as he blew the dust off his glasses and ran his hand through his crew cut, creating a small dust storm that mostly settled back on his head, as the battered two-ton 1946 Studebaker truck was not able to go fast enough to blow it away.

It was July 1957: I had just turned sixteen, and Eli was fourteen. We had been to Meneger's Dam, Santa Cruz, and Pisinimo collecting bags of charcoal made by the Papago Indians as part of a program set up by the American Friends Service Committee to help the tiny villages along the southern part of Papagueria develop a modest economy. The truck was full of the fresh charcoal we had helped dig out of the pits and bag, and a couple of men were getting a ride back to Tucson, displacing us to the back of the truck, a familiar and happy place for us. We had spent the night outside Santa Cruz sleeping under a mesquite tree on an old blanket now padding our bodies as we lay on the charcoal. Eli had helped cook breakfast over a small fire as I explored the desert. The short fences made of dry bushes and branches, sometimes bound together, and never more than twenty yards or so long had always puzzled me. It was clear that they did not bother any range cattle very much, but they were common in some areas of the reservation, especially around small ranchos with dried fields. As we ate our tortillas and beans, the men simply told me that the fences were waiting for the rain. I wondered about that as our old man ground it back into third gear and the truck speeded up to perhaps twenty miles per hour while the July heat beat down on us.

As the sun turned the desert into shimmering mirages we got to Pisinimo. Happily our father pulled up in front of the small store and stopped, and Eli and I climbed down and went to a cattle trough with some green water alive with insects and algae. We splashed the water on our heads, keeping it out of our mouths as we wiped the slime and algae from our hair with our T-shirts. The men stayed in the shade of the truck cab and our father came out with some red cans of a cheap soda pop that he passed to the men, with one for Eli and me to share. As we moved out of town we watched our dust blow around a few women under a ramada with their baskets of scarlet saguaro fruits and large ollas with the fermented cactus juice.

Eventually we bounced up onto the broken pavement of the Sells Highway and headed home as the old man got the truck up to perhaps thirty-five miles per hour. The relatively smooth ride allowed us to look around and consider the large black cloud that followed us, gaining ground. As the cloud overtook us, we could smell the ozone in the air and the peculiar pungent dusty smell of the desert before the rain. The temperature plunged, and suddenly it was cold in the back of the truck. These summer storms were exciting, scary for the lightning but wonderful for the heady smells and rebirth of the desert that followed the rains. Eli and I talked about the smell, as we had been told that it came from the ozone from the lightning, but there had been no lightning. As a huge bolt of lightning crashed overhead, our discussion shifted to the chances of being struck by lightning while sitting in the back of an old truck. We reassured each other that it would not happen, since the tires were rubber, and we sat spellbound watching the lightning dance across the sky and ridgeline in the distance. On cue the rain we had hoped for in Pisinimo flooded down on us. The truck slowed immediately, and we remembered that our father had forgotten to replace his windshield wipers and the desert dust on the windshield turned to mud. The rain was cold and we climbed under the blanket and watched the bags of charcoal appear as the gray dust washed off. Even though it was the middle of the afternoon, the storm was dark enough that the cars speeding up behind us had their lights on as they swept around us.

The truck slowed to a stop. Ahead a wash was flooded with dirty brown water covered with foam and debris. I walked over to admire the impressive debris flow. Sometimes entire dead brittlebush, small cactus, or pieces of mesquite and paloverde would rush by, bouncing over the road. Later I learned that because so many of the desert trees were legumes with symbiotic bacteria that synthesized nitrogen, their leaves were rich with the nutrient, otherwise in short supply. Thus the runoff of water laden with this litter was of great value to all the desert plants. Eventually Gary Nabhan explained to me that those bush fences I had seen had been placed where they would trap the nitrogen-rich debris, as well as the foam in the sheet flooding that followed sooner or later. Then the people pulled up the "fences" that collected the soggy plants full of the rich foam and litter and took them to fertilize their fields. One of his books also explained how the ladies of Pisinimo and their saguaro wine contributed to the rain that was now slowing. I looked up into the clearing sky to see that the old truck was slowly moving past the cars, and I clambered up the side onto the sodden bags of charcoal.

If an impending lightning storm is scary, surely one of the most awesome experiences one can enjoy is being in the back of a slow truck driving through the Sonoran Desert as a storm clears and moves past. The moist smells of creosote bushes replace the smells of dust and plant exudates that preceded the storm. And the desert haze is replaced with air so clean that the distant blue mountains are blue no longer and seem almost on top of us, crystal clear, with the saguaro waving their arms in the distance.

The sun returned and warmed us as we made it to Sells, where we stopped for gas. We stood around the small store and listened to the quiet murmurings of the people talking in their native language. Eventually our father paid for the gas, and one of the men and a woman returned to the cab of the truck, and we moved slowly through Sells. I always liked Sells. The people were dignified while open and friendly, and the many dogs bounding about were enthusiastic about their lives. The day was waning as we approached Tucson and took our passengers to the community near San Xavier. We admired the mission built by Father Kino long ago, now glowing gold in the setting sun. Eli and I replaced the passengers in the cab and drove home.

The trips to Papagueria stopped at the end of the summer, but not before the three of us made many more trips to the area. The many dusty trips, replete with breakdowns of the old truck, flat tires repaired in the desert, the heat, and the summer rains burned the desert deeply into our souls. We spent most of our free time in high school and college hiking in the mountains around Tucson. I had discovered the ocean and a dream of a career in marine biology and even built a scuba outfit with hardware-store pipe and an old B-29 regulator. It almost killed me, but not before I continued the drive through my beloved desert, often going by and wanting to visit El Pinacate, a spectacular lava field in the Sonoran Desert of northern Mexico.

Now, some thirty years later, I sit near a sacred cave high in the Pinacate looking out over this, the Sonoran Desert that defines my soul. I think about Gage and Anaika, my two kids exploring the lava tubes, and realize that they are the same age as Eli and I were that summer of 1957. I look down at the campsite I discovered in 1974 that we return to several times a year. It is a place where I feel at peace and one with my world. Having counted and measured plants and counted pack rat middens, I have a long-term baseline data set that fascinates me because it shows such huge variation in time and space. I learned that the jumping cholla bud production follows a heavy—usually El Niño—rain period with a lag of about one to two years, and the pack rat population that eats the fallen buds follows a couple of years later, and each of these events has a significant impact on the habitat and associated fauna that could not be understood without knowledge of the earlier wet year and lag periods. At larger scales I look out over vast areas of the desert below and can see maybe one hundred square miles of creosote forest, almost all of it killed by the long-term drought. I speculate that it will turn into bur sage, saltbush, and maybe some brittlebush. I can see the area along the road where a dense forest of very tall *Opuntia* cactus has died and is starting to fall over. The cactus forest was so thick it shaded the ground and I used it as a classroom for students to find dozens of species of spiders and reptiles.

Future observers will never know about these very dense and lush creosote and cactus forests that used to occupy this area, replete with all their smells and, more important, habitats for the remarkable diversity of associated animals. We call this collective loss of memory a "sliding baseline," as successive human generations consider an increasing loss of biodiversity to be normal.

The dense mesquite forests in the washes remind me of the extinct Pleistocene megafauna referred to as "ghosts" by noted paleoecologist Paul Martin. I wonder what the habitat was like twelve thousand years ago, when the forests were replete with all the spectacular animals now missing. Clearly the mastodons would have much changed the patterns of the legumes, but what were the sloths and pigs doing to the vegetation? What did the place look like before these animals disappeared? We know from the pack rat middens studied by the ecologists at Tumamoc Hill in Tucson that the vegetation recovered from the ice ages at different rates. I have seen the ecosystem as a teenager inspired by summer rains, and I have observed the significant climate-driven changes through my lifetime, but the species in the desert give no hints of their ice-age histories or of the patterns that one would have seen in the presence of the megafauna.

I look at the small fields along the base of the mountains where the drainages empty, and I remember Gary Nabhan talking of the ancient farmers working those same fields and think back to the days in Papagueria with the Tohono O'odham and wonder how the people have shaped this arid landscape over thousands of years. Their trails and sleeping circles, intaglios and middens are scattered everywhere. As my kids return and we head back down, we talk about how the area with the cave has been sacred to such remarkable people for so very long. We follow their trail marked by modern hikers as well as by pieces of ancient pottery and feel a spiritual bond with those who came to worship at the cave systems we too had respectfully visited.

I am an old man now, on the second day of the annual hike into the Sierra Nevada mountains in California. The first day is not too bad, but the second day is grueling. We have slogged up and over a pass, down into a valley, and are heading up a steep exposed slope. I pause after we move into some deep shade beside a small stream. The rest of the group moves ahead, but I always stop here, along with one of my kids who trails the old man in case he drops. I like this spot because it has a nice patch of corn lilies and tiger lilies that remind me of another time in my life.

I drift back to 1947 as a six-year-old child in a remote and very small Oregon logging camp between the tiny towns of Tiller and Drew. We had a similar stream beside our small shack, and I would lie beside the skunk cabbage looking up through the tiger lilies finding shapes in the clouds, watching the old B-36s lumber by overhead and listening to the log trucks shift down into their "granny hole" as they moved up a hill from the woods. There was a rotting log in the bog, and one day a huge yellow-orange salamander appeared out of the log and scared me. I ran back to get the big axe used for firewood and was lugging it back to chop the salamander to bits when my mother saw me and persuaded me that the salamander was my friend. The salamander was my only friend in the camp, in fact, and I spent the rest of the summer "playing" with her. She came out about 10 a.m. and wandered around the small swamp. I would watch her and other wildlife in the bog, but there was a lot I did not see that summer: I never saw her meet a friend or even eat a large meal. The old loggers told me that long ago the male newts came over the mountain from a different drainage to breed with the females in my valley (and vice versa), but the other drainage had been logged and eroded, and no more newts came. I am always amazed at how these childhood memories become so vivid in the few minutes I rest in the shade with a patient kid. Eventually we struggle into a small area at the edge of a valley, where we make camp and eat and get ready for a difficult climb up over a high ridge.

The next morning we leave as early as we can to beat the sun. It is a steep climb around and over boulders in slippery scree and sand. The group spreads out across the steep slope, each person searching for a good route. The sun peers over the hill and blinds me as it always does, and I slow to lean on my walking stick and pant. My son Gage almost runs into me, lying to me that I am doing great. A few years before I struggled by Anaika, my powerful daughter, who muttered, "You are a tough old bugger, Dad." All parents struggle to teach their kids to be critical thinkers and independent and then suffer through their success as the teenagers apply these talents to their parents. Yet we also dream of earning our children's respect, and being judged a tough old bugger by this young woman makes me happy through the years.

As I panted I thought about being a tough old bugger and I looked at the ancient foxtail pine tree beside me, probably approaching its third millennium. A thin strip of bark wound its way up the gnarled red trunk, supporting a single branch with three blue pine cones. The bark stood out several inches from the rest of the trunk. Elsewhere I once cored some strips like that and learned that the single strands of bark had been growing for over two hundred years, each supporting a single branch. I had been watching many trees at our camp for over twenty years and believe that those blue pine cones are simply waiting, possibly for decades, to have a "mast" year in which they mature and release their seeds. After a millennium a small strip of bark hanging on for hundreds of years supporting a single stubby limb with a few pine cones takes the idea of a tough old bugger to a new level. We finally make it to the top of the ridge and repeat the regular ceremony of breaking out the Sling-Light chairs at a place where we can look over three different valleys in the morning mists and eat smoked oysters from a can.

There is a large cairn on the ridge celebrating a family's history coming into the valley below that they refer to as Elysian Valley. Elysian Valley is a sweeping open valley, but one that is difficult to access. We will camp in Elysian Valley, wondering what the mosquitoes eat the rest of the year, and then move into our normal valley.

The next day we climb back up and hike along the rugged high ridge and drop down into a small cirque valley in the early afternoon. We have been coming to this valley every year since the mid-1980s, when Dick Bray and Al Ebeling introduced us to its beautiful isolated lake. Today we eat some bean soup for lunch and lounge in our comfortable Sling-Light chairs anticipating the *Blazing Saddles* routine. I listen to the relaxed group chatting and ponder the history of this small valley.

Obviously the cirque lake was formed by a glacier, and camped on the moraine one can see the scraped rocks and moraine and understand how it was formed, but what of the ice-age animals that lived in the vicinity? Which of the now-extinct mammals came into the high country? Did anything graze on the willows? Apparently beaver do not come up into the high country, but did mastodons or sloths modify the habitat? Perhaps some of the large ice-age pigs? Did the magnificent short-faced bears, lions, and cats follow prey up this high? Did the Sierra Nevada bighorn sheep come up to escape those predators? The ice-age predators disappeared; the ice melted; the foxtail and lodgepole pines colonized the high country, establishing new timberlines; and the rest of the alpine community moved up into the valley. From where I sit I can see remnants of the ghost forest of tree trunks that had lived several hundred feet above the present timberline when the climate warmed four to seven thousand years ago; in areas where people have not burned them, the old snags, stumps, and logs lie about, still offering the Holocene history in their wood.

We have found artifacts that demonstrate seasonal hunting, but how was the ecological community structured five thousand years ago? John Wehausen, one of the best natural scientists I have met, told me that the Sierra Nevada bighorn sheep have been genetically isolated from the desert bighorn sheep for some 425,000 years (four glacial cycles). Presumably the sheep were safe from humans in the high country, but what was the relationship between the sheep and their predators? Did the people remove most of the deer? What were the main predators? Wolves and wolverines were here; how did they interact with cougars and black bears or coyotes and foxes? Today the black bears dig roots in the high meadows and kill young deer, but probably not adults, and certainly not sheep. John Wehausen believes that naturally cougar populations are linked with deer. The wolves are gone, and the wolverines are, if not gone, extremely rare, but Roland Knapp tells me of a 1929 report of a wolf and a wolverine. Were there so many coyotes in the system when the other predators were there, and what were the relationships between wolves/wolverines, coyotes, and the now-missing Sierra foxes? In other areas wolves displace coyotes and release foxes. Perhaps the loss of the wolves/wolverines explains the large population of coyotes we see today, and this in turn contributed to the disappearance of the Sierra red fox.

What of the aquatic systems? The lakes would have been full of yellow-legged frogs, and tree frogs would have been common, preyed on by garter snakes and raccoons. A wonderful diverse assemblage of zooplankton and benthic invertebrates would have characterized those fish-free lakes, and in turn these may have supported large populations of the now-rare water shrews and perhaps other aquatic predators. What of the fish in the streams? Roland Knapp, the Sierra biologist struggling so hard to save the yellow-legged frogs, told me that the spectacular golden trout evolved from an ancient anadromous salmonid isolated behind waterfalls and lava dams, while the fish below the dams eventually became the modern rainbow and steelhead trout. Thus our spectacular golden trout may offer important genetic histories of an important line of trout.

The discovery of gold in California was the beginning of major changes: Miners swept the state, destroying vegetation in the mountains, controlling and rerouting most of the drainages to use the water for mining and drinking water. Many of the other high lakes are still dammed, but the lakes in "our" valley were never dammed. However, the mining activities certainly involved the removal of vast amounts of wood; the slopes near the mining operations were virtually clear-cut. In most areas there would have been seasonal flocks of sheep feeding the mining communities and devastating native bighorn sheep with introduced diseases. The shepherds tending the sheep would have used the ancient downed trees for campfires, while their sheep denuded the vegetation, virtually eliminating the tiny pine seedlings. In addition, the shepherds were alert to the value of transporting fish into the lakes for food during their summer visits. The predation by the fish render the yellow-legged frogs virtually extinct in these lakes. This assault on the frogs continued almost to the present as the Department of Fish and Game transplanted trout into most of the lakes.

By the late 1800s most of the damage to the natural habitats had been done, and by the turn of the century, hundreds of people took Sierra Club outings. These early visitors were not low-impact campers: They relied on a great many horses and mules and set up elaborate camps, with their guides feeding them deer and trout. They and the large herds of stock must have had considerable impacts on the high country. And by that time people were introducing exotic trout to the lakes and streams, so in most places the golden trout originally introduced into the high country were in turn replaced by and interbred with the rainbow trout or by the predaceous brook and brown trout, thus further endangering the yellow-legged frogs. It would seem that everybody loves big trout in lakes where they do not belong, but how many people care about a wonderful tough species of alpine frog?

As I sit here, happy to be back, I contemplate how lucky it is that this little lake survived most of the trauma. It is too small and isolated to have been ravaged for firewood or abused by sheep or Sierra Club outings. We have attempted to quantify the amount of dead wood and tiny pine recruits in as many valleys as we can in our area, and our little valley has by far the highest density of ancient downed wood, indicating that except for the occasional packer who comes in with a power saw, the Holocene record recorded in the old trees is largely intact, as documented by Tony Caprio, an excellent National Park Service ecologist. In addition, this area seems to have been spared the grazing and trampling of pack animals, and it has orders of magnitude more tiny seedlings than other areas we visit.

However, fish had been introduced, and when we first came the yellow-legged frogs were found only in the shallows or in the small meadow below. Roland Knapp, the great frog biologist struggling so hard to save the yellow-legged frogs, told me that the State Fish and Game personnel consider the fish in our lake the only pure golden trout stock left, but we are pretty sure there are rainbow in the lake as well. At any rate, the introduced chytrid fungus and the introduced fish have virtually eliminated the spectacular yellow-legged frog, and now it seems that the genetically pure golden trout may be gone as well.

Finally, in 2009, for the first time in over twenty years the pines opened their cones and released their seeds. This year the place is a cacophony of Clark's nutcracker, responding to the mast year. Sadly, we see that beetles have killed most of the seeds spared by the birds, so the success of the masting effort depends on the birds caching live seeds. There are other subtle changes afoot as well. When we first came here, alpine chipmunks were relatively common, as were the pika in the rocks. Now, however, both are rare here. Jim Patton, one of the best mammalogists in the West, has revisited Joseph Grinnell's surveys from the early 1900s. He has found that the warming and reduced snowfall associated with the climate changes has moved some of these species farther upslope, but in our case, and probably in most others, there is no habitat for them, and they are quietly disappearing. This is the sad case of modern extinctions: Species such as the alpine chipmunk, pika, and yellow-legged frogs simply become rare and then disappear, often not missed except by dedicated naturalists like Roland Knapp and Jim Patton—and by amateur naturalists who pay careful, loving attention to their own backyards and special places.

How do these vignettes of personal history relate to the science of ecology? In my day job I am a marine ecologist and have done my own research in very different habitats than these extreme terrestrial habitats—much of it under water. But ecosystems are complex and dynamic, and the fortunes of the species wax and wane on vast scales of space and time—from microhabitats of a few centimeters to large regional patterns of many kilometers, and from days to months, centuries, or even millennia.

My own research has focused on the coastal ecology of several rather different habitats, among them rocky coasts, kelp forests, and Antarctic sea bottoms. My most important insights have come from efforts to consider the dynamics of plant and animal communities at many different scales of space and time, and from many years of observing organisms in the field. Good community ecologists can identify the important or strong interactions in an ecosystem and focus on studying those relationships. But such insights depend on a genuine sensitivity to the large-scale natural history, the really big-picture understanding that is a product of integrating many types of knowledge—especially history, climate patterns, and life history biology. Whatever the habitat, one must not only assimilate a wide range of historical and scientific literature, but also invest a great deal of time in the field in order to acquire a meaningful feel for the system, the sense of place so essential to any good ecological understanding.

In my own case an early familiarity with the regional archaeology and the Tohono O'odham and their relationship to the Sonoran Desert helps me picture the early human impacts, from hunting to farming. My lifelong respect for the spectacular programs of the Desert Laboratory on Tumamoc Hill in Tucson have given me some hints about the Holocene history of this system. But mostly my sense of place simply reflects a great deal of time spent with the plants and animals and people of the Sonoran Desert. Similarly, early experiences in Oregon logging camps and wilderness areas preadapted me to respect and understand the alpine habitats of the Sierra Nevada. At the same time, an understanding of this area has to be built on some knowledge of history, especially the mining history of the late 1800s.

But this is not enough: I believe one must actually see, feel, and contemplate ancient but still living bristlecone or foxtail pine trees to truly appreciate their tenacity for life. And to appreciate the dual nature of their physiological resilience as well as their extreme vulnerability to human-related disturbances, one needs to be with their babies, the small seedlings and saplings over a couple decades during which they are buried under snow for consecutive years, to measure the very slow growth rates of these small trees and to see some die. There is simply no substitute for actually experiencing nature, to see, smell, and listen to the integrated pattern that nature offers an open mind.

The tales I've shared are my own, but I suspect that all successful community ecologists have similar personal histories in which they have developed that special feel or sense of place for a particular system. It is clear that this sense of place is critical to their scientific success.

My concern is that the modern trends in both families and education are to eliminate these experiences in nature. Families no longer spend quality time outdoors, and the educational systems from kindergarten through graduate school have not only eliminated field experiences from instruction in all levels of natural history but also even eliminated respect for those biologists who study classical biological material. There is a strong trend to bring parts of plants and animals into the laboratory and to model rather than actually experience and respect nature itself. Today young scholars are asked to study ecology without any sense of place, any understanding of the actual organisms living in real environments characterized by their important histories. An intuitive sense of place so necessary for an integrated understanding of living systems must come from personal experience—smelling, feeling, and seeing the important relationships.

Lessons from 763

I cradle the sleeping wolf in my arms, keeping her warm against the morning frost, the way I held my daughters when they were small. However, anything but small, wolf number 763 is a sturdy, eighty-pound, lactating female. Mid-May, denning season in the northern Rockies, the snow only recently melted; she has not yet begun to shed her luxuriant winter coat. I help state wolf biologist Kent Laudon fasten a radio collar around her neck, fitting it carefully, smoothing her thick black fur so it doesn't become tangled in the leather strap. I smile, glad at the good fortune of having a young alpha female step into our trap. These are the best wolves to collar, the ones who can tell you most about the pack, the ones most likely to live long, stick around, and not disperse, taking your collar and data along with them.

We trapped her in Glacier National Park, Montana, in the valley sculpted by the North Fork of the Flathead River, in an aspen stand next to Johnson Meadow. (I have changed the meadow's real name to "Johnson" here to protect the wolves who den there.) Covering ten square miles, the meadow held several aspen stands and a long-abandoned homestead, now little more than a few boards weathered silver and a midden heap in a damp declivity. Low-lying glacier-smoothed mountains rimmed the meadow. Anaconda Peak's rocky south face rose sharply above a series of soft green ridgelines that fade into the north. To the south, Huckleberry Mountain's rounded bulk breached a fog bank, its shoulders a mosaic of burned and unburned patches.

When wolves (*Canis lupus*) recolonized northwestern Montana in the 1980s, they chose Johnson Meadow, a secluded opening in a sea of lodgepole, as their first home. In 1986 renowned wolf biologist Diane Boyd, then a graduate student, confirmed the first denning activity here after a sixty-year human-imposed wolf absence. Glacier National Park administrators keep this place closed to the public but occasionally allow researchers in—and then only when the resident Dutch pack, which is radio-collared, travels away from the den. Trouble is, the wolves seldom leave, lingering at the den site until long past spring whelping season, feeding on the abundant deer and elk with which they share the meadow. When they do leave, they tend to travel one or two miles from the den, remaining in the general vicinity to hunt or rest with their pups at areas called rendezvous sites.

The aspen's pale green leaf buds are just beginning to open that morning as I work with Laudon and his field crew, all of us coordinating our efforts to handle 763 as gently and efficiently as possible. She stands there, trapped, but watching us impassively as we approach with a needle loaded with the anesthetic that will enable her to sleep through what follows. Laudon deftly jabs the wolf's thigh, and then we wait for fifteen long minutes for the drugs to work. She lies down gradually, wobbling a bit, her head going down last. When she is completely out, he releases her foot from the padded leghold trap. Only as we carry her to the tarp where we would work on her do we notice her swollen nipples. She has pups nearby. We blindfold her and speak in whispers so as to not disturb her sleep as we draw blood, check her sharp, white teeth, her body condition (which is superb, even for a new mother), and listen to the drum of her strong, steady heartbeat. I estimate her age—three years old and in her prime.

The collar always goes on last. After we finish fastening it, I continue to hold her, waiting for the anesthetic to begin to wear off, keeping her warm with my body, because the drugs we have given her impair her ability to regulate her body temperature. I lower my head and smell her fur, which carries the sweet, clean scent of woods and river and deep, deep wildness—a wildness so primal I have no words for it. Humans have long feared what we can't understand. Part of my work as a scientist involves trying to understand wildness. I pick up one of her front paws and hold it flat against my palm. It is bigger than my outspread hand.

She takes a long time to awaken. Eventually I feel the smooth muscles over her ribs contract. One of her ears twitches, reacting to some sound audible only to her. We ease her off the tarp and onto a soft bed of new spring grass. As we prepare to waken her fully, I offer thoughts that she live long and well, that she birth many strong pups in her lifetime, filling this meadow for many generations with their howls and wildness, and that she steer clear of trouble. She has an official number, but before we release her I give her another name: I call her Nina, after my mentor, Nina Leopold, who has helped deepen my understanding of the work of her father, Aldo Leopold. He was among the first to recognize the ecological value of wolves. Laudon injects her with an antidote that will reverse the anesthesia completely. Within five minutes the wolf rises, turning back to look at us as she leaves. Her amber eyes burn into mine before she vanishes into the shadows at the edge of the meadow.

I thank the wolfen Nina for the data she will give me, which will illuminate the effects of keystone species. Her collar's steady stream of high-quality location data—which produce one fix every three hours, with an error of plus or minus one meter—will tell me the story of how she is influencing elk behavior and how this in turn is shaping patterns in this landscape. She will show me how wolf presence affects everything, from the way aspen grow to songbird diversity to mycorrhizal fungi. I chose to focus my PhD research on aspen because although it is the most widely distributed tree species in North America, it has been declining in large portions of the intermountain West since the 1920s. Aspen reproduces clonally, sprouting from extensive root systems, and provides critical habitat for diverse species of wildlife and plants. It is the second richest type of temperate terrestrial habitat in North America; only riparian zones are richer in biodiversity. Because aspen can support such profligate biodiversity, its decline has created pressing research and conservation needs. I chose to study elk, because their impacts on aspen are greater than those of other ungulate species. The steepest aspen declines have occurred in areas of elk winter range, linked to predator removal, disease, and climate change.

My wolf research is based on the concept of trophic cascades. The term "trophic" refers to anything related to the food web, while the phrase "trophic cascades" refers to the movement of energy through the community food web when predators are removed (or when they return). This dynamic resembles a waterfall and involves top-down regulation of an ecosystem, in which predators have a controlling influence on prey abundance and behavior at the next lower level, and so forth through the food web. Remove a top predator, such as the wolf, and elk grow more abundant and bold, damaging their habitat through vegetation consumption that is excessive and unsustainable (called "herbivory"). Intensive herbivory can lead to ungulates literally eating themselves out of house and home, and consequently to loss of biodiversity and destabilization of ecosystems. Ecosystems that lack top predators can support fewer species, because the trees and shrubs that create the habitat for these species have been overbrowsed. With top predators in them, they contain richer and more diverse habitat, and thus can support a greater number of species such as songbirds and butterflies.

Cycling predator and prey populations leave marks upon the land. My work involved paying close attention to these marks. The hallmark of natural history, this sort of attentiveness has long inspired and enabled classic work on predators and their prey by scientists such as Aldo Leopold and Olaus Murie. In terrestrial ecosystems with large carnivores, one of the most blatant marks predators and their prey leave is the "recruitment gap." When wolves abound, elk stay on the move and become more vigilant due to fear of predation. They spend less time feeding, which can enable browse species to persist until they are above browse height. To measure the effect of wolves on Johnson Meadow, I was measuring tree ages, and also songbird biodiversity. I was comparing this to sites that had no wolves, to see if a difference existed between them in how trees grew, or in the number of songbird species.

Trophic cascades are integral to the keystone approach to conservation. In 1969 marine ecologist Robert Paine created the phrase "keystone species" to apply to sea stars (*Pisaster ochraeus*), which functioned as top predators in the rocky intertidal zone he studied on the Washington coast. There, on a rocky crescent of shore, he took sea stars from the rocks and hurled them into the ocean. In his control plot he did nothing. As he continued removing sea stars from the rocks, the assemblage of species there gradually began to change. Within one year, the sinister implications of his experiment became all too graphically obvious. Where *Pisaster* flourished, so did the vegetation. Where *Pisaster* had been removed, the mussels took over, crowding out other species, eating all the vegetation, until little more than a dark carpet of mussels and barnacles remained.

Paine's keystone concept is fundamentally about species diversity—that the presence or absence of one key species influences the distribution and abundance of a great many others. This metaphorical term, which refers to species that function similarly to the keystone of an arch (remove the keystone and the arch falls apart), was intended to convey a sense of the unexpected consequences of species removal. Processes driven by keystone species include nutrient cycling and seed dispersal. Research can help us recognize these losses and thereby act to prevent others. Natural history lies at the heart of this research. By observing and recording relationships between predators and their prey we can help shed light on the value of keystone species—and help conserve them.

Four months after I collared Nina, it is August, and I am in an old-growth larch forest surveying her den—a new den she dug last spring into a south-facing hillside, about a mile and a half from the ancestral den the Dutch pack has used for all but a handful of the past twenty-three years. Her collar data suggests that the pack is no longer near either den. It is one of those glorious late summer days in the Rockies, sunlight shafting through the forest, silhouetting the blown seed heads of fireweed and grasses, the larch needles just beginning to turn. I shed layers, enjoying the gift of this day. As I measure vegetation, I catch a quick black blur in a nearby huckleberry thicket—a wolf, checking us out. I try radio-tracking, but fail to pick up a signal. My field crew and I hurry to finish. This encounter bothers me, because I make every effort to have no contact with wolves as I gather plant data, to avoid disturbing them any more than necessary. It may seem paradoxical that someone who collars wolves would avoid encountering them, but it is one way that I try to minimize the impacts of my research on this community.

We pack out our field equipment and bushwhack away from the den, moving west into the meadow, traversing it on a labyrinth of wolf trails through waist-high ochre grass. Eventually we find the primary wolf trail, which is wider than the rest and meanders through this landscape like a river. Johnson Meadow seems no less primordial than I recall, with bones everywhere and wolf lays—patches of flattened grass marked with wolf scats—that indicate where the pack had rested. Besides my field crew, my companions on this fine day include Glacier National Park carnivore biologist John Waller, fire ecologist Dan Donato, and his wife Melanie Stidham, a forest ecologist. Waller is here to learn more about my research and offer advice, and Donato to help me parse out the meadow's fire ecology and differentiate it from wolf effects on the aspen.

All at once, just inside the conifers hemming the meadow to the south, we see a wolf, and then another, and another—seven in all, mostly black. Wolf pups, now almost the same size as adults, but nevertheless identifiable as pups because of their curiosity and awkward movements. They lack the grace and elegance of their elders. They coyly peek out at us from behind lodgepole pines too absurdly spindly to provide much cover. We stop in our tracks and watch in astonishment. Waller and I exchange looks. One of the pups beds down in a patch of violet asters, fifty yards from us. One of its siblings follows suit. Another one starts chasing a butterfly. Then it dawns on us that they are not at all disturbed by our presence. Waller nods. We watch them silently for a few minutes and then continue on our way, weaving through the tall grass, leaving a wake of leaping grasshoppers. As I walk on, I reflect on the day I collared their mother, how I held her to keep her warm, how she must have returned to her den that day smelling of me. And I realize the pups and I are no strangers to one another.

We move toward the ancestral den, located in a stand of aspen that graces a low knoll, to examine how a trophic cascade looks in an area of such high wolf use. When we get there, we sit at the edge of the aspen amid the detritus of wolf life—elk bones cracked in two by the wolves' sharp carnassial teeth, the marrow thoroughly sucked out, a mauled plastic soft drink bottle the pups used as chew toy. The aspen's coinlike leaves, tinged yellow, shimmy in the breeze as we discuss the marks left on this landscape by wolf presence, such as the flush of aspen growth that occurred when wolves returned here in the 1980s. I note abundant signs of ungulate presence—piles of elk and deer pellets deposited in the grass and among the aspen—even though this place represents the inner sanctum of wolf activity in the North Fork.

We eat lunch and talk about how all things are connected, and how events that occurred nearly a century ago, when this site was homesteaded, are plainly written on the landscape today: a midden heap, wolves removed by settlers, the resulting explosion in elk numbers leaving ecological artifacts such as the missing aspen age classes and the heavily scarred bark on the older trees. We talk about the stories housed in this meadow—the history of enough wolf lives to repopulate northwestern Montana, stories that substantiate what Aldo Leopold taught so long ago: "To keep every cog and wheel is the first precaution of intelligent tinkering." This meadow shows that many of the habitat degradation and extinction processes precipitated by the elimination of wolves ninety years ago are reversible. Experiencing landscapes like this, where keystone predators rule and all ecological functions driven by them are present freely, inspire one to try to sustain these interactions beyond protected federal lands.

According to conservation biologist Michael Soulé, "trophic cascades science provides copious evidence for concluding that the unpredictable, devastating, downstream effects of apex predator removal are major drivers of global ecological collapse." Strong words. Yet these cascades continue to be controversial in scientific and management circles. While most scientists accept their existence, many are caught up in scholarly arguments about the details of how they operate, the validity of the keystone concept, whether top-down or bottom-up forces prevail, and whether one can make cross-ecosystem generalizations about these phenomena. These arguments are highly relevant. However, because of how rapidly we are losing the wealth of species native to ecosystems it is important for policy makers to move beyond these arguments and begin to apply trophic cascades principles to conservation and natural resources management.

In the century since we created the science of ecology, we have learned and generally agree that ecosystems are complex and multicausal. We also agree that the world is changing rapidly, due to climate variability and the human population explosion. Conservation biologists John Terborgh and Jim Estes consider loss of top predators from ecosystems worldwide due to persecution by humans a crisis as significant as climate change. They suggest that as with climate change, the problem of loss of biodiversity caused by loss of keystones will only worsen until we take measures to correct it. While restoring keystones will not solve all our problems, it will create more resilient systems, help restore and maintain biodiversity, and heal some of the damage we have done to this Earth.

I continued my den survey that August, working into September at the historic den in the center of Johnson Meadow. I never saw the pups again. Now it is late autumn, the aspen have shed their leaves, and a scrim of fresh snow dusts the mountains. The memory of that late summer day, the pups watching us and us watching them back in wonder, comes to me as I analyze my data. The columns of numbers on my computer screen ineluctably show the mark of the wolf's tooth on the meadow's ecology: Their return in the mid-1980s has changed so much. These data demonstrate that wolves are an essential part of the web of life. Wolf presence has indirectly made aspen and shrubs grow again after many years of overbrowsing by ungulates and has improved habitat for songbirds and elk. And five months after I collared her, the data from Nina's collar is coming in clear and true, providing a line of incontrovertible empirical evidence to support my vegetation and songbird data. Predictably, her collar data spins the story of what it means to be a wolf and how her wildness can mend the web of life and enable other species to live well. She is a keystone—the shaping force that reforms ecosystems into wholes. And her revelations fill me with hope.

Notes toward a
Natural History of Dams

I've never packed a dictionary on the trail, but if I had, I might have saved myself from years of struggle over how people separate themselves from nature. And I would have understood much earlier that dams are as much a part of natural history as rivers.

Infamous Glen Canyon Dam in Utah and the largest dam in the world, Three Gorges in the People's Republic of China (PRC), aren't considered "natural." Instead, huge hydropower projects epitomize humans' control of wild rivers and their ecosystems. Most of us tolerate dams as necessary for electricity production and flood control; some people love them. But there are no books titled *Field Guide to Dams of the American West*, and nobody maintains species accounts or life lists of these concrete behemoths.

According to *Merriam-Webster's Collegiate Dictionary*, the primary definition of "attend," the verb form of "attention," involves "applying the mind to an object of sense or thought." Most people interested in nature might prefer a field guide over a wordbook, yet both tools provide the "who, what, and where" answers that one must first decide on before proceeding toward matters of "why."

But when I look in *Webster's* for clarity I find that dams could fulfill all four definitions surrounding acts of mindful observance, the main task of any ecologist. For example, dams could demand that we "apply the mind to an object." Attending to dams might involve a "selective narrowing of consciousness and receptivity" or invoke "observations toward action." One of the dictionary definitions of "attention" even implies that we become aware of dams with "sympathetic consideration of the needs and wants of others."

As a fledgling field naturalist some thirty years ago, I was taught to pay attention to nature, not people, and certainly not dams. Exploring the rivers of southwestern China taught me otherwise.

Consider a river in China that has remained undammed for a thousand years. The job description of this watercourse is daunting—to cut through the wall of the world's highest mountains and escape to the distant sea eighteen hundred miles away.

Those mountains are the Himalayas, and that waterway is the Nujiang, the "Angry River." The Nu tumbles off the Tibetan Plateau and rages due south through China's Yunnan Province, carving a trench deeper than any canyon in North America before sinking into the hills of Myanmar and Thailand, and, finally, the Indian Ocean. The Nu remains the longest undammed river in mainland Southeast Asia.

I first visited the Nu in 2005 at the tail end of the summer monsoon. The river surged with whitewater and chocolate-covered standing waves large enough to swallow a big rig truck. I couldn't keep track of the number of rapids; the river cast a spell, pulled at my power to think clearly, as if it wanted to replace my normal consciousness with something wilder.

But I wasn't in the Nujiang to tally rapids. I was there to attempt to understand dams. China has already constructed more dams than any other country and the Nu holds the promise of adding additional megawatts to the PRC's burgeoning power grid. Before Beijing declared a dam-building moratorium in 2004, plans were afoot to erect thirteen new hydropower projects on the Nu. By the time I arrived, it was said that this number had been reduced to four. But even four dams would tame the Angry River.

I am not a connoisseur of hydropower projects; my professional training has focused on the details of ecosystems and crafting policies to protect biodiversity. I was initially attracted to Yunnan because so much of biological importance is at stake. With only 4 percent of China's land area (about twice the size of California), Yunnan has more plants and bird species than all of North America. The United States harbors about 8 percent of the world's mammals; Yunnan alone provides habitat for close to 6 percent. Yunnan is a naturalist's dream, a spectacular center of species richness. And within the province there are biodiversity hotspots *within* hotspots—the Nujiang is one of them. In the river's upper watershed, biologists have discovered so many species that it's as if one out of every three mammals and birds in the entire United States were crammed into an area about the size of Arizona's Grand Canyon.

I am biased toward biodiversity, but I learned quickly that the Nu is also a cultural hotspot. Of the fifty-six officially recognized ethnic minorities in China, twenty-five groups have their homelands in Yunnan. Nine of these minorities, each with a distinctive language, dress, and set of cultural customs, make their living in the Nu. Within hours of entering the valley, I encountered Lisu hunters, Nu pastoralists, and Tibetan trekking guides on their home turf. Many of these people don't speak Mandarin, and most of them make less money in a year than I do in a couple of days, but all of them were welcoming.

Visiting backcountry Yunnan, with its poverty and lack of basic services, is challenging. And, like minority peoples worldwide, villagers in the Nu have little say in decisions affecting their livelihoods. The proposed dams fall into this category.

With no huge hydropower projects built yet on the Angry River, I attempted to visit a dam construction site on a river that neighbors the Nu. That's where I discovered that the Chinese (like most of us) can easily choose to see only what they want to see. If we must "selectively narrow our consciousness and receptivity" while we sort through multiple incoming impressions, how do we properly choose between what is important to attend to and what is not?

The dam site was close to a small city, so I assumed it would be easy to access. I also knew that the government considers such sites closed to public scrutiny. But the project was almost complete, and I had seen pictures of it posted on the Internet. I figured that taking a taxi would look more "official" than riding a bike, so I hired a driver and set off.

Sultry, subtropical heat mixed with rank humidity rising from the river. The water was slow-moving and brown, with upstream erosion bleeding off hills bearing small-scale rice paddies and rubber plantations. Shimmering heat rose from the road, and waterbirds fished shoreline shallows.

Just as I heard the first faint din of heavy machinery, the road was blocked by a checkpoint. Three white-gloved guards sat at a table in the shade; they stood as my driver slowed and stopped.

I don't speak Mandarin, and the driver and the guards knew

no English. Nonetheless, communication in China is usually not a problem. I smiled and gestured upriver toward the construction site, clearly audible in the distance. The guards did not smile. The leader peered at me intently, then slashed his arm down at an angle to the ground: "No." In Beijing, you can loiter at a building site all day watching sky cranes play a giants' game of pickup sticks, lifting huge bundles of industrial rebar, but not in Yunnan, not on a river at a dam site where most of the power to be generated has already been sold to Thailand, with few benefits left for the local people.

Chinese hydrologists select data from dam impact studies that fit predetermined political preferences. Each of Yunnan's three great rivers flows beyond China into Southeast Asia; all Chinese dam studies portray downstream impacts as inconsequential. Every report attends to the possibility of environmental problems, but in the studies I've read, the authors never find any.

It's always a challenge to separate observation from interpretation, yet I find this case of selective attention to be particularly revealing. Throughout four millennia, the Chinese have never split the world into the binary categories of "nature" and "culture" that we employ without a second thought. There is no "wilderness" in classical Chinese philosophy, language, or contemporary conservation and development practices. The Chinese replace these with *Wu Xing*, the Five Elements—earth, fire, water, air, and metal—what a scientist would label "biodiversity," or an economist might describe as "ecosystem services." But today on Yunnan's rivers, the political drive for development is so strong that even an ancient framework that places people squarely in the mix discounts nature *and* people. There are so many multiple dams planned for these waterways that riparian ecosystems will be replaced wholesale with a series of slackwater reservoirs separated by massive concrete bulwarks. Poor farmers will benefit little, while power companies stand to gain great wealth.

I retreated from the checkpoint guards and walked back down to the river. The distant thrum of construction was replaced with the slap of small waves against the weedy shoreline. The river smelled rank in the hazy sun, and my thoughts were full of fish, birds, insects, water plants, and the monsoonal flows that bind life to life in subtropical southwest China. Human consciousness and memory are always selective, but because of my expanded sense of natural history, I can no longer look at a bird or take the pulse of a river without accounting for the soil that slips downslope from a farmer's field, the fish that are gathered from the current, or the megawatts that pulse through power lines away from the source toward distant cities.

Natural history is a supreme antidote to abstraction; what we choose to pay attention to makes all the difference in the world. My predilection is to attend to flowers, birds, and river flows, but I know in my bones that dams are part of nature, too. Beavers build barriers and a free-flowing creek becomes a drowned forest, a swamp. Human engineers erect dams across watercourses and a river is degraded, wild no more.

When I teach natural history, I always introduce beginning students to the relativity inherent in observations—"Is the bird you saw bigger or smaller than a robin?" "What role does the distance from water play in your attention to eddies lined with cattails, the adjacent gallery forest, and a bamboo thicket perched on a terrace at some remove from streamside?" The same observational rules apply to dams. Compared to towering Douglas-firs, we identify coast redwoods as the tallest trees in the world. In the Nujiang when they are completed, Songta and Maji dams, at 1,000 feet and 984 feet, respectively, will become two of the highest dams in the world. In contrast, the Liuku dam will rise only 118 feet.

Reservoir length is a diagnostic field mark with important ecological consequences for river species. Maji reservoir will drown over twenty miles of the Nu; Yabiluo reservoir will be less than three miles long. These artificial lakes will certainly impact the thirty-three species of endemic fish in the Angry River, but few people know the details, since all dam studies are "state secrets."

The tons of concrete poured into hydropower structures are roughly analogous with an animal's body mass, since the bulk of a dam is similar to body mass. Songta just edges out Maji dam in sheer size using this field mark. Biologists like numbers—percentage of this plant population in flower, young birds successfully fledged versus number of eggs laid. Comparing dams on the Nu, you can figure the number of rural people displaced per dam. This calculation does not correlate with height or mass of the dams' headwalls; of the fifty thousand citizens likely to be relocated by all these projects, the largest dam, Songta, will only be responsible for 7 percent of the people. Maji Dam will force the relocation of 38 percent of these rural farmers.

One can also collect life history data on dams. Unlike squirrel or monkey populations, however, the birth and death rates of hydropower projects are not easily quantified. No engineer knows the rate at which silt will build up in the Nujiang reservoirs. In China, there are no models to predict the effects rising temperatures due to global warming will have on land use patterns and erosion rates in these watersheds.

The natural history of dams nudges us toward active sympathy for the needs and wants of others. Who are these "others," and how do we attend to their "needs"?

To address these questions in the Nu, I began to focus my examinations using simple arithmetic. I added up all the power expected from all the dams. For the Nujiang, this equals about 23,000 megawatts (MW) with thirteen dams, some 13,000 MW with four. I did the same math for the Nu's mighty neighbors, the Lancangjiang (Mekong) and the Jinshajiang (Upper Yangzi). The PRC plans to build eight dams on the Lancang; when complete, these structures will generate about 16,000 MW of electricity. For the Jinsha, the upstream reaches of the Yangzi, the figure is at least 35,000 MW.

Confronting these abstract numbers, I needed a metric to put all this power into perspective. The megawatts generated from all three rivers' dams is equivalent to some 75 percent of all the hydropower produced today in the United States. And still, this latent capacity is overwhelmed by China's insatiable demand for electricity.

Regarding "needs," there is one additional life history trait concerning these three rivers: Villagers are utterly dependent on them in their free-flowing state. In the Nujiang, it is not clear where villagers can be relocated to since most arable land is already under cultivation. On the Lancang, 60 million people harvest freshwater fish from its waters. Downstream from Yunnan, some 40 percent of all the animal protein consumed in Cambodia comes from this river. For the Jinsha, an equivalent ecosystem services data point surrounds the river's contribution to the water supplies of 300 million Chinese as it flows into central and eastern China to become the fourth largest river in the world.

Paying attention to people and nature together is tricky business. If I'm careful to account for every impacted species, the numbers and geographic range of populations are startling. There are endemic fishes that swim in limited areas and fishes that occur over thousands of river miles, forest fragments that hold some of the last primate populations in China, and migratory cranes and other waterfowl that are completely river-dependent. The ethnic minority peoples in the Nu matter, and they are joined by many other groups living along the Lancang far beyond China southward down to Vietnam's Mekong Delta. Most of the people who drink water from the Yangzi are Han Chinese living at a great distance from Yunnan. Certainly, the corporate hydropower executives and provincial and PRC government officials who control all the decision-making around the dams must be tallied, though they live scattered from Bangkok to Beijing.

The UN is in this mix. If the climate forecasts of the Intergovernmental Panel on Climate Change are accurate, the Tibetan Plateau headwaters of Yunnan's rivers will warm more rapidly than almost any other place on the planet, and the glaciers that feed the Nu, the Lancang, and the Jinsha will melt into thin air sometime after 2050. So we can include in our considerations of the natural history of dams the U.S. president, India's prime minister, and the other 180 country leaders grappling with how to control carbon emissions. The climate in western China is heating up due to CO_2 emissions, and a warming world creates a host of local and regional problems that can only be solved with international action.

Sensing the world, selecting out information, acting with sympathetic consideration—these are the skills of any field naturalist. Paying attention is the oldest human practice—and the most difficult when we remember that there is no "us" and "them," only "we." China's rivers and dams have helped me understand this message clearly.

In Yunnan, at the end of a long day walking at dusk beside

a strong brown river, I notice a single slack power line strung between my path and the channel. I recognize the field marks of two poles of influence with two price tags to consider, along with two sets of vital needs: water in the river and light in the night. These choices may appear to be in conflict, but look deeper. How close do our activities fit within the flow of rivers? How far off? In natural history, we can see patterns that connect and those that separate us out, just as in Yunnan there can be some hydropower development but not an endless number of dams. Flowing water bestows many gifts, and rivers can bring good fortune only when people act within their means.

Talking to Wild Things

You would think me mad were you hidden along my path in the Sandia Foothills. I talk as I walk.

"Hey, Kingbird. Good catch. You got that one."

"Well, hello, Baby Asters. You sure are looking pretty today."

"I see you up there, Rock Squirrel. Be careful or a hawk will snatch you up."

"Run, Whiptail, run!"

Aldo Leopold wrote that we needed to become plain members and citizens of the land community. To me, that means you need to know who lives in your neighborhood, or in the neighborhood you are passing through.

Leopold also wrote that there are those who can live without wild things and those who cannot. As one who cannot, as one who loves wild things, I want to know them.

The path that leads to knowing your wild neighbors is natural history.

Whether it is biologists more comfy in a lab than outside, more used to looking through a microscope than through binoculars, or outdoors folks zipping over hill and dale on mountain bikes instead of stooping to befriend a wildflower, too many overlook and underthink wild things.

Given that Lord Man has created a mass extinction of wild things, it is a must that more of us know wild things, and know them as neighbors. It is easier to kill those you do not know or to take away the homes of those you do not see than kill or take over the homes of those you do know—those whom you know as neighbors and fellow citizens.

We must pay attention to nature to keep other Earthlings from harm.

Eyes of the World

Your job is to find what the world is trying to be.

—WILLIAM STAFFORD, *"Vocation"*

On a gray New England day, serenaded by clanking radiators, I sat with two dozen college classmates in a basement biology lab. Hunching over microscopes, we examined bits of greenery.

On the stage of my scope lay the feather-shaped frond of a fern. Along its pale green underside, the frond's projecting fingers were studded with brown, BB-sized dots. As I turned the focusing knobs, each dot gradually resolved into a mounded cluster of tiny, translucent umber globes, glowing faintly under the scope's bright lamp.

Before taking this introductory botany course, I had never turned over the foliage of a fern, never noticed the intricate structures that decorate specialized fronds. Now, despite the unfamiliarity of new terms and concepts, studying plants was beginning to feel like coming home.

My first two years of college had been fraught with ambivalence. Lacking confidence in my training and aptitude, I initially shied away from the science classes that intrigued me. Instead, I sought fulfillment in music and activism, friendship and romance. Soon I was spreading my energies so thin that no one pursuit brought satisfaction.

But all the while, there was running through my days another sort of extracurricular experience—a private, inexorable one that I never thought of as pertinent to my education: I noticed and felt my everyday world with great intensity. A walk from dorm to classroom down a leaf-scudded sidewalk on a late-fall day, past chittering squirrels and doorway cats and strolling crowds, could fill me to overflowing with sensations and questions. The quality of light slanting through a dining-hall window, the scents of a grimy working-class neighborhood where I bought groceries, the clatter of a subway car out of subterranean grit into a golden winter afternoon—I found these more provocative than the formal features of my college life.

At the time, this turn of mind didn't strike me as an academic asset. In childhood, I'd often been accused of oversensitivity; in college, my tendency to be stirred by such a wide range of stimuli seemed an embarrassing liability, a romanticism that distracted me from concerted learning. I couldn't seem to discover a bridge between my sensory suggestibility and a recognized course of study. I often found myself more interested in being than in doing—a predilection unlikely to land me on the dean's list.

What I couldn't yet appreciate is that the capacity to simply *attend* is a great gift. It can give rise to creativity and joy as well as intellectual engagement; it can foster a life of reverence, compassion, and useful work. But to reap such rewards, one must learn to temper wonder with knowledge, curiosity with method. And here, one of my first teachers was the underside of a fern.

As I set to work in the botany lab that autumn afternoon, I knew that each of the minute capsules clinging in rounded clumps to my scrap of foliage contained countless spores—

microscopic fern factories. Ferns are more primitive than flow-ering plants and cannot produce seeds. Instead, they play out a two-stage reproductive process. First, the plants we normally recognize as ferns release spores, which land on the earth and develop into stubby, inconspicuous plantlets. Wherever fern plants grow and multiply, these low-growing proto-ferns also appear—though at three or four to the linear inch, they're easy to overlook.

Every plantlet produces both eggs and sperm cells. If the ground becomes moist enough, the sperm begin to swim egg-ward, like sperm the world over, toward a rendezvous with fer-tilization. Each successfully mated pair of sex cells then grows into a young fern plant, which eventually develops spore-bear-ing structures—and the cycle begins again.

The course instructors required us to sketch everything we observed in the lab. It didn't matter, they assured us, how well we could draw. They simply wanted us to look long and hard enough to make visual notes. I'd always envied people who could translate their seeing with artful precision into lines, shapes, and shadows on paper—and while I didn't imagine I could ever join their ranks, I was intrigued by the explicit permission to draw without regard for artistic ability. So I scrutinized the clus-ters of spore capsules that clung to the fern's nether parts, trac-ing their contours on a notebook page. Absorbed in that delicate caress, I channeled awareness from eyes to hand to paper. To my surprise, the resulting sketches bristled with life and, if not scientific accuracy, at least a pleasing authenticity.

As I stared, the scene under my microscope came to life. A puff of what appeared to be brown smoke materialized in the air over the frond, momentarily obscuring my view. At first I was mystified, then it dawned on me what must be happening. One of the tiny capsules, drying in the heat of the scope's lamp, had burst open to release a swirling cloud of near-weightless microscopic spores. As the first puff of spore-dust began to disperse, another appeared nearby. Soon, one hollow capsule after another was letting loose. Miniature pandemonium broke out under the magnifying lenses, spore-clouds exploding like popcorn all over the smoking brown field of the microscope stage. If my hearing were acute enough and rightly tuned, I wondered, would the room fill with wild and unfamiliar sounds?

In their native habitat, those spores would disperse on the slightest current of air, gradually settling over a broad swath of ground; some would eventually give rise to a new generation of ferns. In the lab, another kind of germination was taking place. I annotated the growing sketch in my notebook. And as I watched and drew and wrote, along with the shifting whorls of fern futures that danced beneath my gaze, a quiet but insistent happiness began to bloom. Witnessing the fern's display, I entered into a state of alert, focused presence. My senses sharpened; my mind clarified; my body became serene and awake. I associated such attunement with long walks, with dabblings in poetry and calligraphy and other private ventures. Now, finally, I was experiencing it in a classroom.

That an event of such seemingly modest proportions could engender this happy state, and that I should remember the moment so vividly thirty years later, attests to the potency of natural history study—not only as a way of learning how life works, but as a path to fuller living.

Some of the quiet joy I felt in the lab that day arose from a welcome restoration of humility. The college I attended had a long history of hubris and self-congratulation, and an institutional cosmology that placed human affairs at the center of the universe. At the onset of an epic blizzard that beset New England during the winter of my junior year, one administrator intoned in response to a reporter's question, "Harvard never closes, not even for an act of God." (Divine intervention or no, the university did indeed shut down for several days a short while later.) Here under my microscope was an elegantly orchestrated phenomenon, one of a myriad, that had been playing out around me all my life—and for millions of years before humans showed up on the planet. In pointing to an ancient, intricate world that extended profoundly beyond my own small self, the fern's display offered a refreshing perspective.

And while it's true the plant had no need of me, we were, nevertheless, kin. Fern-gazing offered a glimpse into universal, elemental life processes that link human beings with every other organism on the planet. To witness such events in action is to be reminded of one's membership in the community of life. Nature at close hand offers a lesson in both the simple logic that compels so much of biological activity—Be fruitful and multiply—and the staggering complexity entailed in carrying out that imperative at the level of cells and molecules.

Such complexity invited inquiry. What mechanism caused the spore capsules to burst open under the heat of the lamp and propel their contents outward? How much heat was required? How many spores swirled in each of those minute dust-clouds, and why such abundance? Did other forest creatures use the spores—make them into fertilizer, eat them for lunch? In the woods, how far could a single spore travel? How many spores might succeed in dividing and developing into proto-ferns, in turn creating new fern plants? I could see no end to the lines of inquiry uncoiling from the drama playing out on my microscope stage.

In pursuit of questions like these, nature study encourages a lively resonance between direct observation and secondhand learning, between organism or ecosystem and teacher or text.

It also trains the curious observer to move supplely along an investigative spectrum ranging from rigorous research to imaginative speculation. In order to find what the world (to borrow Stafford's phrase) is trying to be, we have to come fresh to every observation. To study natural history requires us to set aside preconceptions, to be tutored by the world. Yet even as a student of nature learns to get out of the way, she must also bring her own intuitive sensibility to the project.

Geneticist Barbara McClintock, for example, credited her Nobel-winning discoveries to "a feeling for the organism." And science illustrator Jenny Keller points out, "If you're trying too hard to screen out the personal while you're drawing a bird, you're likely to screen out some things about the bird." Biologist and longtime bird-watcher Todd Newberry goes so far as to argue, in *The Ardent Birder*, that the art and science of watching birds, "for all its skill and paraphernalia, is at base an emotional enterprise." He published this book about his avocation in order to "share not only a skill and craft but also a state of mind—more, a state of heart, one akin to love."

For me, college botany became a gateway to the naturalist's path. Emboldened by the excitement of my sketching sessions in the botany lab, I eventually took a couple of drawing classes—where I learned that practice and instruction could compensate for my lack of native skill. Sketching became a way of shedding preoccupation, of slowing down and inhabiting the moment. It remains one of my favorite tools for learning. In the decades since I first scrutinized a fern frond, I have spent countless hours with notebook and pen, being tutored by plants and bugs and birds, by deep forests and botanical gardens and rushing mountain streams, and by the human companions with whom I have visited those settings. As a teacher, I have enjoyed passing along this practice to children, teenagers, and adults.

Yet as enlightening and compelling as informal natural history study may be, a nagging voice in my head sometimes asks whether it makes sense to continue indulging in this activity, in a world that's coming apart all around us. The question can be especially acute for sporadic amateur naturalists like me, whose discoveries are unlikely to save imperiled species or habitats, protect water supplies, or improve the practice of agriculture. Can we nature dilettantes really afford our dalliances? After all, when there is less and less of intact "nature" to observe, isn't it less important to attend than to *do* something?

But that's ultimately a fruitless question—and a false dichotomy. I believe we might as well ask whether there is still time for reverence, for gratitude and celebration, for music and education and art. The survival of viable ecosystems and the creation of sustainable human societies depend as urgently on the attitudes we cultivate as they do on our activism. Our children and grandchildren will never heal the world, nor perhaps even feel compelled to try, if they fail to develop empathy and respect for the beauty and diversity, the complexity and interdependence, of all life. And they are not likely to get there without exposure to adults who model such appreciation. They need opportunities to meet nature head-on, whether in a biology lab or a school garden, along an urban lakeshore or on a mountaintop. They need encouragement to pay attention and to wonder.

I watch my university students at work outside the gates of the teaching garden they built, making compost. Two of them grasp opposite sides of a large wire-mesh sieve framed with wooden boards, moving the contraption vigorously back and forth between them. Their classmates shovel chunks of material onto the sieve from a Dumpster-sized bin, where food scraps, garden clippings, and manure have been keeping company with fungi and bacteria and bugs. In two months' time, the bin's contents have undergone a fecund transformation, surprising the novice composters in the group. Although these students have been told that bacteria produce heat in the process of breaking down organic matter, they're unprepared for their first contact with an active compost pile. Some reflexively pull their hands back as their eyes widen: The pile has more than doubled in temperature, rising to 140 degrees Fahrenheit.

In the final compartment of the long divided composting bin, the corn husks and apple cores have disappeared. The wheelbarrow beneath the sieve fills with rich, moist grains, as dark and pleasantly aromatic as coffee grounds. The sifters run it through their hands with satisfaction; one brings a fistful to her nose and inhales. Another student wheels the compost through the garden gates and helps dig it into a new bed, to nourish the broccoli and eggplant and basil that will eventually grace the community dinner table. These students are learning not only to pay respectful attention to natural cycles, but also to work together, tending the Earth in exchange for its gifts. In their bright eyes and easy movements, I see the pleasure of their growing erudition and community spirit, their fruitful intimacy with an ancient cycle that's as intriguing and essential and common as dirt.

Long belittled by academic scientists as a quaint, old-fashioned diversion, nature study should occupy the core of any twenty-first-century school curriculum. Rachel Carson anticipated this argument in 1952, when she accepted the Burroughs Medal for her book *The Sea Around Us*. "If we have ever regarded our interest in natural history as an escape from the realities of the modern world," she told those gathered at the award ceremony, "let us now reverse this attitude. For the mysteries of living things, and the birth and death of continents and seas, are among the great realities." In *Silent Spring*, Carson dramatized how military-industrial societies disregard and degrade those realities at our peril.

A highly educated woman I've known and liked since childhood is married to an architect who works on large commercial projects. This friend once told me that her husband had been hired to design a high-end shopping complex for a prosperous midwestern suburb. When I asked her to describe the site where the project was to be built, she gazed at me blankly for a moment, then replied with a dismissive shrug: "Oh—it's just empty land." She didn't mean that the tract held no soil or water or topographical features, that no plants, birds, mammals, insects, or other organisms interacted on it—only that the area had not yet been turned to direct human use. A global society increasingly peopled by humans who think this way—that is, the society in which we currently live—does not stand a robust chance of survival.

Reclaiming nature study in schools and communities would be one fine way to heed the sage advice penned by Robert Hunter and sung by the Grateful Dead: "Wake up to find out that you are the eyes of the world." We are the eyes of the world. And we urgently need to see anew.

One of my dearest friends, a writer and former botanist who has found a midlife calling in religious leadership, recently observed that, like me, she was chastised as a young girl for her "oversensitive" nature. "I spent my whole childhood thinking that 'sensitive' was a bad word, like 'stupid' or 'ugly,'" she wrote to me, "and I was totally ashamed of that label. And then—miracle!—that childhood 'curse' turns out to be the gift that lets you love the world and all its wonderful, astonishing beings with a wide-open heart. Your heart. My heart. All of our hearts. Breaking all the time, and somehow still, if we are lucky and can stand it, going back out to love the world and heal it in the only ways we can."

I don't doubt that there are thousands of young people wandering around neighborhoods and schools at this moment, perplexed by their own unique brands of "oversensitivity"—intellectually adrift, unable to find a match between their passions and the curricula on offer. I suggest that we provide them with microscopes and binoculars, a field guide and a fern, a notebook and a pen, a raised bed in which to plant some flowers and food. Let's give them a chance to find what the world is trying to be.

The Gardener Gets Arrested

Speeding between raised beds this morning, doing a hasty job of weeding the beans and pinching tomato vines, I went to turn on a faucet and nearly squashed a praying mantis. She was perched on the spigot handle, and before I even saw her she gave my finger a sharp pinch. I jerked back and cursed. Stifling an urge to whip out my pruners and cut the mantis in half, I took a deep breath and looked down at her.

The mantis waved her tarsi in the air, ready to fend off the next flesh that threatened her. She cocked her triangular head—the model for so many sci-fi alien faces—to get a better look at me. Alert, poised, she held herself as still as a stick and waited. The unsettling thing about praying mantises is how they watch you. Most wild creatures—small or large, swift or slow—will hide or flee at the sight of a human. It's their wisdom, and our sorry karma. But not the praying mantis. The mantis will stand her ground, trusting in her cryptic behavior—her stillness, camouflaged coloration, and sticklike mimicry—to remain invisible to predators and prey. But she knew I saw her, and she was ready for me.

Arrested, I settled down to watch her more closely. Her raptorial graspers, those wicked-looking barbs on her tarsi, are for snatching and grappling onto prey. Those mandibles can bite through the bones of mice. Her five eyes—two big compound globes that can see colors and images, and three smaller ones that see just shades of dark and light—can dial in prey with remarkable precision, and she'll eat just about anything she can seize, including a mate if she didn't have a decent meal prior to coitus. I especially admire the ootheca she can excrete as a protective covering for her eggs. The size and shape of a cat turd, it's stiff and spongy as Styrofoam. In winter I often find oothecas plastered to branches, or in the woodshed stuck to the pieces of lath I use for garden stakes. The hatchlings and several stages of nymphs are all miniatures of the adult, maybe a tad cuter.

A flock of chickadees fluttered past just then, distracting me, and when I returned my regard to the mantis, she was gone. Her swift return to invisibility made me smile. With plenty of chores still to be done, I got back to work, but as I thinned the lettuce seedlings, I tried to be more careful and watchful, more mindful of the company. I was also more relaxed, in a better mood, more present to the world—all of this a gift from my session with the mantis.

When I'm hiking, camping, canoeing, I'm always on the lookout for insects, birds, reptiles, mammals, interesting plants, rocks, seeds, scats, tracks, or cloud formations. I relish my recreational encounters with nature, and I try to smartly observe the daily lives of the animals and plants I meet. But I'm even more likely to encounter nature when I'm working in the garden, when I'm out stabbing nature with my spade, whacking nature with a hoe or a scythe. I go to my backyard to wrestle with nature, to make nature say vegetables. When I'm working in the garden, I'm attentive, but selectively, so I see what I'm looking for quite clearly, but I'm utterly blind to most everything else. Unless, that is, a wild creature arrests me. Unless something unusual penetrates my willful concentration, punctuates my headlong, purposeful equilibrium. Then, the little world I'm attending to stops, and bulges into mystery. A chickadee! A centipede! A snake! The unexpectedness of small animals is part of their charm. They are not my quarry. I'm not seeking them out to add to a life-list. They aren't the answer to my bird- or bug-watching intentions. They are free agents, in no way bound to my will. They are suddenly just *there.* Inexhaustibly interesting and ultimately unknowable, they are abundant, everyday epiphanies.

Epiphany—from the Greek, meaning a *showing forth,* an appearance, like the sudden manifestation of a god, an arresting experience that triggers a radical reordering of one's sense of how the world works. And don't animals provide that all the time? Like yesterday's garter snake, basking invisibly on a gray flagstone—until I wandered too close, whereupon it uncoiled and blazed forth as sudden as a bird, and disappeared into the grass. Every snake I see blazes with its own strange presence. And with an epiphany comes recognition that, even as we are strange and mysterious to one another, we are all related. Snakes, birds, insects—all are due courtesy and compassion.

There's certainly no guarantee that a gardener will be either ecologically aware or given to compassion. But if those virtues are worth cultivating, gardening can be one of the most effective ways to cultivate them. The more I can learn about the sex lives of insects, the feeding habits of chickadees, the denning preferences of garter snakes, the better my chances for a bountiful harvest. And while working in the garden, there is always potential for arresting experiences, for those nose-to-nose encounters with other creatures that reveal my kinship with all creation.

I'm partial to watching local insects because I *can*. Insects and I cross paths every day. It is so humbling to look at the eyes of a house fly and see both something familiar—"Those *are* eyes"—and absolutely alien—"but I have no idea what seeing with them is like." Meeting any wild creature face-to-face, I can feel its otherness, and recall my own animal nature. And insects are especially good for such encounters, because insects—in contrast to, for instance, polar bears or white rhinos—are often close at hand.

For fifteen years I worked as the gardener for the county courthouse in the center of our town, a focal point and gathering place for the whole community. The sidewalks leading to the front doors of the courthouse were flanked by rows of hybrid tea roses. In this most public landscape, I did everything possible to avoid using any toxic chemicals. I planted roses that were resistant to disease, so I didn't need to apply any fungicides. But aphids were tougher customers. Just as the roses formed succulent buds, aphids would materialize from nowhere. And close on the heels of the aphids would come a bevy of my fellow citizens. The grounds of the courthouse were a bit of a fishbowl, with lots of foot traffic into the courts and county offices, and visitors to the jail. So I was the beneficiary of a lot of unsolicited gardening advice. And nothing elicited strong, quasi-knowledgeable opinions more than aphids-on-roses.

Sometimes the aphids would totally glove the rosebuds, and I would resort to smothering them with soap sprays. But I eventually discovered that the best ploy for controlling aphids was to give them a starring role in a new story. Aphids, of course, are a food of choice for ladybugs, but I really hadn't paid close attention to how ladybugs actually preyed on them. Once I started observing more deliberately, I noticed that the ladybugs would appear in great numbers two to four days after the aphid peak, and within another few days the aphids would be reduced to stragglers. I also discovered that the ladybugs liked to lay their eggs on the leaves of crocosmia that grew around the base of the maple trees. When one of my volunteer supervisors would exhort me to spray, I'd come back with a story. "I know what you mean about these aphids. But we've got a complicated situation here. Aphids are the primary food of ladybugs, and I really like ladybugs, don't you? So if I spray poison on the aphids, the ladybugs won't have anything to eat, and they just won't stick around. So, look here . . ." I'd lead my fellow citizen over to a crocosmia, lean down and, with a magician's flourish, tip up a leaf to reveal the neat rows of little yellow silos glued to the underside. "Ladybug eggs!"

If a curious child came by, I could usually locate ladybug nymphs, like miniature alligators with orange pinstripes. Even plain old aphids are interesting creatures if you look closely—dollops of lime Jell-O with tiny red eyes. I always had my 10× magnifier in my pocket, and whenever I pulled it out to inspect the roses, someone would come up beside me and lean in alongside.

"Whatcha looking at?"

"I'm looking at these juicy little bugs. They're quite beautiful. Want to take a look?"

"Cool!"

Close encounters with wild nature, in my experience, often trigger a complicated range of responses. Fascination. The thrill of intricate beauty. Maybe a touch of horror. Joy. Or that ringing stillness I associate with awe. But also grief, remorse, bitterness. It is exactly there, in my complex emotional responses to other creatures, that I discover my sense of relationship. Whenever I am fascinated by the spiral pattern of seeds in a sunflower, agog at the power of salmon leaping up bludgeoning cascades, or horrified by the possum eating its road-killed sister, I am feeling the tug of my ties to everything else in the continuum of life. My intellectual belief in kinship is confirmed by the feelings that arise in immediate experience. And there I discover a sense of responsibility. How should I behave toward birds, snakes, insects?

Even if there can be no real communion between me and a praying mantis, how about compassion? The mantis has an appetite like mine. Its tarsi are rather like my fingers. And, oh, how I would love to be able to see the world through a compound eye.

Senses of kinship and compassion aren't likely to trigger a saintly withdrawal from all killing. However mindful of nature's ways I may try to be, I'm still going to end up with blood on my hands. Creatures are going to die under my rototiller and hoe. Plants that would grow here in my absence are going to get rooted up if they don't fit into my vision. But the more I can understand the lives of everyone else, the more judiciously I can care for the health of the whole. A gardener—aware of the furious round of birth and death in the soil, in the bushes and woodlots, in the air above—can only try to be mindful of his dependence on other lives, and try to be a conduit of humility and gratitude. Learning the lifeways of the creatures in my garden can help heighten my awareness and lessen my ignorance. I can learn to grapple with "pests"—kill some as painlessly as possible, relocate some, cope with others—without anger. And I can wish for the prosperity of the tribe of slugs, while defending my lettuce seedlings with a hoe.

I study the natural history of critters to be a better gardener, maybe even a better citizen. I grow flowers and food for their salacious beauty and salutary grub. But just as essential, I garden to get arrested, to be taken out of my solipsistic self by the singing of a frog or the dazzling overflight of geese. Natural history helps me understand how all creatures try to meet their needs in the ceremony of appetite, just like me. And cultivating a knack for getting arrested keeps me open to the complex reality of the mantis, the garter snake, the humble aphid.

Music and the Natural World

The life of a touring musician is a strange one. Not for him the security of the nine-to-five schedule, the steady income, the pension, home every night with the family. Unless he is like Celine Dion playing in Vegas, or Andy Williams in Branson, Missouri, where the audience comes to the artist, he must travel in order to perform. This is true of classical, jazz, folk, and popular musicians the world over, and it's been that way since the time of the troubadours, at least. On the face of it, it is an easy life—performing an hour or two a day. Where's the hardship in that? Friends who come on the road for a week to get away from the office imagine some sort of vacation distilled from glamorous scenes backstage at Rolling Stones and Madonna concerts. They are shocked to find themselves exhausted after three days, and unable to keep up. The travel is grueling, preparation for a show takes hours, dressing rooms are usually spartan and filthy, and travel is numbing and tiring.

So how do musicians survive, and even get to enjoy the nomadic life? To counter the boredom of travel, and the stress of performance, musicians have traditionally resorted to drugs and drink, and maybe that will work for a while; but there comes a fork in the road, and down one fork lies the Grim Reaper, and down the other survival. Most who choose survival have a strategy to keep themselves sane and sober(ish)—and it usually involves other interests. A musician of my acquaintance knows just about everything about the French Revolution and scours the bookshops of the world for obscure classics on the subject (this passion has overtaken his previous obsession with tall ships). Another studies the railways of the world and is particularly keen on the diesel engine. Yet another sets up an easel on the tour bus and paints. For my own predilections, it might be necessary to look back a little . . .

I grew up in North London, right next to the wondrous Hampstead Heath, a great lung on the edge of the city, where my friends and I would frequently play. As urbanites, this was our freedom and experience of nature, and we enjoyed it as much as the cinema, TV, or a good board game (one friend went on to become a zoologist). The other nature experience was the summer holiday, where I could run free for a couple of weeks by the Scottish seaside, and wonder at red admiral caterpillars, run through ant swarms, and capture hedgehogs. All this time, I was too lazy to learn the names of most of the things I encountered. The world of music then became my overpowering interest. This is predominantly practiced indoors, usually at night, and is fueled by several pints of beer. Sleeping all day is considered by some to be a professional necessity. I would still ask the names of passing birds, but the information would usually slip from my small and addled database. Birds of a different plumage—miniskirts, Ozzie Clark boas—seemed more alluring. I suppose I lacked a nature guru, someone who could take me a little further . . .

In my twenties, my escape from the doldrums of travel was reading, but as I hit thirty, the family gardening gene kicked in, and I actually began learning names of plants. About this time, I was fortunate to team up with Simon Tassano, my tour manager/sound engineer, who was and is a committed bird-watcher. On days off, he would suggest small diversions to nature reserves. The first one we visited together was in the Swansea Estuary, between Port Talbot and Swansea in South Wales, one of the most polluted industrial areas in Britain. It seemed impossible that the natural world could exist there, in sight of towers belching fumes and flames, docks, filth—indeed, one of the abiding memories of the place was the dead frogs, thousands and thousands of them underfoot, their sensitivity to environment rendering them vulnerable to something in the atmosphere. Aside from that, the place was teeming with wild-life, and after a visit to Peter Scott's Wildfowl Centre at Slim-bridge, I was hooked. After that point, looking out the window of the car/van/bus became a more focused activity. Was that a kestrel or a sparrowhawk? If I'm in Hawai'i, what's that java sparrow doing here? How can a tree support the weight of that many rainbow lorikeets?

Also in the 1980s, I began working with bassist Danny Thompson, which just added to the fun. Danny was also a bird lover, and we would spend New Year up in northeastern Scotland, watching for eiders, guillemots, razorbills, and gan-nets. He took a couple of years off from touring in the 1970s to make wildlife documentaries with John Aspinall, who took the profits from his casinos to fund Howletts and Port Lympne zoos. Danny was famed for getting in the cage with the tigers (hence "Tiger" Thompson), had a son working at London Zoo, and loved all things to do with nature. It was a wonderful feeling to know that I was with like-minded people, who loved the same things and loved to be in the same environments.

You never know how kids are going to turn out. My youngest son, Jack, started picking up insects at about age two, and never stopped. He developed a large beetle collection, and insect fairs became a regular date on the family calendar. He wrote a child's guide to insects of the Santa Monica Mountains. To keep a parallel interest, I collected butterflies. In order to encourage this budding entomologist, I thought it was time for the family to go somewhere tropical.

One spring, while Jack was still young, we took a couple of weeks in Costa Rica. At La Selva, we saw howler monkeys, peccaries, and a sloth on the ground (they come down every week or so to defecate). On the Osa Peninsula, we saw toucans, scarlet macaws, spider monkeys, squirrel monkeys, hundreds of species of butterflies, tanagers—so many beautiful moments on that trip. One of my favorite memories is of the Los Angeles cloud forest, a small reserve not far from San José. We took a short self-guided hike that ended at a hummingbird feeder, where about a dozen beautiful species were coming and going. For my wife, this trip was a turning point in her appreciation of the natural environment: To hear her and my son and myself all gasp at the appearance of our first violet sabrewing hummingbird was very special. This is a large hummingbird, purple and black, with a long curved beak, and it is an understatement to say it has a presence. Our idea of a family holiday is now a nature holiday, and we've since been back to Costa Rica about five times, and visited other parts of Central America and the Antipodes. On a recent Costa Rica trip, we stayed at the Organization for Tropical Studies research center at Las Cruces and were allowed to assist with the ringing of birds. We were able to examine many species at close range, some that were normally hard to see in the rainforest. It was a great thrill—one of the thrills of my life—to hold and release a violet sabrewing. The birds are netted in a mist net—almost impossible to see even if you know it's there—and then taken to a central work station set up in the forest. Here they are weighed, measured, and tagged, and a blood sample is taken. Before being released, it takes the birds a little while to regain their equilibrium; the old conjuror trick of throwing the doves into the air won't work here. So they must be held on a flat palm for ten seconds, thirty seconds, a minute—and here you are with this precious jewel on your hand, this pinnacle of the beauty of nature, its iridescence, which is just a flash as it might fly past you, now inches from your eye, trembling ever so slightly as its inner ear recalculates up and down, left and right. Meanwhile, my heart is soaring as a bird soars.

Perhaps we become more complete musicians as we become more complete human beings, by letting ourselves be absorbed into the natural world, instead of trying to impose ourselves upon it, or creating an artificial world in which to live. I believe observing nature has helped me to develop a sense of time and place in song—singing about the senses puts the listener into the scene and into the present tense, a valuable musical shortcut when you only have a few verses to get your point across.

My son Jack is now seventeen, and the music gene is kicking in hard, so although he is still a naturalist, it may not be his career; but I hope that if he ends up as a touring musician, he'll be looking out the window from time to time, checking out the red kites on the A40 near Oxford in England, or using that day off in Perth, Australia, to walk through Kings Botanical Garden, which starts off manicured and watered, and ends up as bush, wild, and dry, with miles of banksias, parrots, and echidnas.

What a privilege to travel the world and have chances to escape out into wilderness, or, if stuck in a city, head for the zoo or the park. Life on the road is grueling, but at any moment the fickle itinerary may drop you within range of something beautiful, transcendent, and moving.

Becoming a Neighbor

Rise up nimbly and go on your strange journey
to the ocean of meanings.
The stream knows it can't stay on the mountain.
Leave and don't look away from the sun as you go,
in whose light you're sometimes crescent, sometimes full.

—RUMI, *translated by Coleman Barks*

Jalal al-Din Muhammad Rumi, the thirteenth-century Sufi poet and mystic, counsels us to be aware that life is a journey toward meaning, a strange journey that we have no choice but to pursue. And in our travels through life, we are changed, "sometimes crescent, sometimes full." From childhood through young adulthood and eventually to elderhood, we slowly come to understand more about the world and our place in it and are transformed by that understanding. Our stories, then, are in fact narratives of our travels, both internal and external, and the meanings that they help reveal to us. Everyone has such a narrative. This is mine.

It is ironic that my life's journey began at the sea. I am at home on land, be it desert, rain forest, or mountain. I resonate at a deep level with the life that is rooted in soil and with the animals that make their homes there. Over the past fifty-plus years I have slowly grown my own roots on land to become a more permanent citizen of the places where I have lived and raised my children. But it began for me at the sea, or at least, at the edge of the sea, and it's there I need to begin to tell my story about how my relationship with the natural world, my becoming a neighbor, came to be.

The San Francisco Bay Area was an interesting place to grow up in the late 1960s. Apart from the obvious, culturally historic reasons with which everyone must be familiar, it was also the time and place where I became aware of the world around me and what I wanted my place in it to be. I started seventh grade in a new school with patterns that differed dramatically from those at my elementary school. Instead of having just one teacher who tried to cover everything, my day was now divided up among several teachers, each of whom only taught one thing. Some of them were unremarkable, at least judging by my grades, and some were effective, judging by my eventual ability to go on to college and a life as an academic ecologist. But one teacher in particular was outstanding. Mr. Peter Kimball, seventh-grade science. It was with him that my journey toward meaning began.

At least, that's what the school called the class: seventh-grade science. Mr. Kimball called it Marine Science. He had some notions that, in retrospect, I imagine were considered odd for their time. Notions that science shouldn't be taught disconnected from the natural world and that learning would be more meaningful to kids if it was connected to the place where they lived. Since we were only a few miles from both the Pacific Ocean and the San Francisco Bay, it made sense to him to build his science curriculum around the sea. Just as the marine realm integrates and regulates many of the world's great systems and processes—climate, water cycle, the evolution of life itself—so too can it integrate all of the ways we can look at the world, which (broadly speaking) was supposed to make up the seventh-grade science curriculum of the time.

Yet Mr. Kimball's odd notions went further than that. He believed that to know something about how the natural world worked, kids need to get to know the natural world itself. To get out there, to get wet and dirty, to turn over rocks, and to make friends with limpets and algae and sea gulls. It is almost impossible to believe, looking back on it now through the lens of modern norms and practices dominated by budget constraints and fears of liability and litigation, but Mr. Kimball took us on nearly twenty different field trips to the tide pools north of Half Moon Bay. It seemed like every time there was a really low tide during school hours, we'd hop into a bus and go out to spend some quality time in the real world, at the edge of the sea.

Yet his notions did not end even there. Up to this point, I've only described a really creative teacher who was willing to push the limits of what a school administration would allow. What made him truly unique—and what led to the start of the transformation in my relationship with the natural world—was what he expected from us.

Mr. Kimball did not ask us merely to appreciate being out of doors. Certainly, we did appreciate it; all of us enjoyed our time hopping around the tide pools far more than we enjoyed sitting in the classroom. But on our trips we were expected not simply to enjoy being in the presence of nature; we were expected to get to know it, in detail, like a scientist might. We made collections of algae, preserving them using standard herbarium techniques, and identifying them to species. Even after all of these years, I still remember more about the algae of the California coast—*Fucus, Egregia, Ulva,* and dozens more—than I remember from most of the classes I took in college. Our default textbook was *Between Pacific Tides* by Ed Ricketts and Jack Calvin, and with it as a guide we learned about chitons (my favorite being the gumboot) and barnacles. We laid out hundred-meter tapes and collected data to reveal patterns of intertidal zonation. We invented devices that would let us collect water samples at specific depths below the surface. We even had a final field exam where we had twenty minutes to find specimens for each of the items on a list, named only by genus and species, and then to take the specimens back to where we found them.

It was exciting and I loved it. And looking back on it now, I think I have come to understand why. It was the first time in my life that I had been treated like an adult. Nature was not just a place to play in; it was a place where I could dive down into the details of what made a place what it was. And more, I was *encouraged* to do it, *expected* to do it. He didn't ask if I was up for it or offer it as an extracurricular enrichment exercise. He didn't ask if I was *interested* in going a little bit deeper. He knew that even for a group of twelve-year-olds, our engagement with the natural world did not have to rest comfortably with only a superficial relationship with the plants and animals that lived in the tide pools we explored, a relationship that could easily have gone no further than a simple "Look at the pretty rock," and "Notice how some of the seaweed is green and some is red." He knew we were capable of *knowing* and discovering new things to be known. Of exploring for ourselves who lived where and why. Of what their names were (and thus following ancient human tradition and tapping into the archetypal power of being able to "name").

And so it is that I can say that my journey toward meaning began at the edge of the sea. My rites of passage out of childhood and into adulthood were, in many ways, defined by my awareness that nature could be known. The other-than-human world was deep and vast, and the more I knew, the more I uncovered what there was still to be learned. But even more, I discovered that I could be in relationship with nature in the same way that I could be in relationship with my brothers, or my friends, or the familiar surroundings in my house and neighborhood. I wasn't a stranger or a visitor to that one place in nature. I knew the beings that dwelled there. They became familiar friends, and I was rewarded for that by being treated with a level of dignity and respect reserved for adults.

By the time I entered college I had spent a good part of every free day hiking and climbing in the Sierra Nevada Mountains. In fact, I remember more about the times I spent in the wild than I do of the time I spent at my parents' house. "Home" became an amorphous concept; wherever there was a big expanse of wild landscape, I was at home, and I simply continued to behave as I had learned from Mr. Kimball: Get to know who else lives in the neighborhood, and why. Trees and birds, mammals and fish, butterflies and beetles—I tried to get to know them all. It's simply what neighbors do. Something very fundamental was growing in my heart, and although I wasn't able to name it until many more years had gone by, I responded to its tug.

A psychologist might look at all this in a more analytical light. Perhaps I was simply following patterns that I had been rewarded for as a small child. Personally, I doubt this. There were many things I was rewarded for when I was younger that now hold no interest to me: I had been an altar boy, a high diver, a Boy Scout, and a woodwind player, all of which I had eventually let go of with no regrets and no sense that I was somehow moving off my destined path. But something about being *in* nature and *of* nature felt right.

Fast forward through a series of educational and personal benchmarks: university, graduate school, postdoctoral research, marriage, children, and tenure as a college professor in both biology and environmental studies. All of them were wrapped around a core of engagement with the natural world. Unfortunately, I had allowed this engagement with the natural world to slowly, imperceptibly be transformed away from an intimate relationship with the landscape through which my journey toward meaning passed. While my enjoyment with the familiarity of nature remained, something about my relationship was incomplete. I felt this incompleteness quite clearly even at the start of my career as an academic, but it wasn't until some years later that I was able to see what was missing.

In the process of composing a life, the natural world had become a subject, scarcely more than the raw material from which I crafted my career. Simply put, I had allowed it to become separate from my spirit. And I had allowed my sense of spirit— that which gives me a sense of meaning and purpose, a sense of right and wrong, a sense of my place in the order of things—to become separate from the natural world.

The problem was simple. I engaged with the natural world through my work, but because I work as a scientist and educator, and because of the normative values placed on those professions regarding emotional detachment from the focus of our studies, over the years I had come to craft my engagement with nature as objective and neutral. Familiar, yes, but largely unemotional and certainly devoid of anything that might suggest unprofessional religiosity. I believed that my profession asked me to treat other species as subjects and not as neighbors, and I complied.

Conversely, I engaged with my sense of spirituality through traditional religious pathways, traditional in a classical Western sense, in which one focuses solely on the human condition and on an afterlife rooted in an "elsewhere" and that views the natural world as a temporary home filled with lesser beings meant for subjugation. Neither mode of engagement—objective natural science or anthropocentric spirituality—was in balance, and considered together they were clearly discordant. I cannot say how it was that I finally became able to articulate for myself this schism in my life, but I was ultimately able to open the door to the next part of my journey: integrating the separate parts of my life to create a whole.

The solution to the imbalance in my life turned out to be simple. I needed to come back into communion with nature as a citizen of the natural world, and not just as a scientist, and I needed to embrace more fully what that communion required of me. I first needed to shed a sense of spirituality wedded to an "elsewhere" and reclaim the sense of belonging and meaning I had discovered as a twelve-year-old exploring the tide pools on the California coast. The other-than-humans I study and about which I teach had to become, once again, beings with whom I was in deep relationship: my neighbors and even my family. I remain a scientist, an ecologist in the classical, academic sense—the sense of it being simply the study of the relationship between organisms and their environment—practicing my craft as objectively as I can, but now with the knowledge and memory that the *why* of what I do is fundamentally grounded in the subjective feeling of who I am within the broader community. This community includes humans, to be sure, but it includes everything else as well: trees, insects, fungi, and birds, all connected in ways described less by asymmetrical utility and more by the relationships that bind us all together.

The details of how I came to this understanding are not really important. Suffice it to say that it involved discovering like-minded people who, through their own diverse paths, have come to create a distributed network of friends and family whose sense of spirituality is grounded in this world, not an "elsewhere," and who are aware of their connections and responsibilities to all life, not just human. We gather regularly, out-of-doors, engaged in simple yet deeply moving rituals that affirm our connection to the web of life. These rituals and our conscious presence of where we are help to clarify for me my sense of meaning and purpose. To be sure, within this network of humans nature sometimes serves simply as a metaphor for amorphous concepts; for example, water is merely a metaphor for flexibility, softness, and flow, and the appearance of a great blue heron represents beauty and grace. But mostly the natural world represents itself simply as it is. Water *is* water. The great blue heron wading along a shoreline *is* a single great blue heron, playing its part in the community of organisms that live in and around the lake. While we are together, we are a community of humans that coexist with all the other beings that live where we have gathered, and this ability to coexist and to understand what it means to coexist defines our sense of right and wrong. By living with these people in the conscious presence of the natural world, I found a way to bridge the divide between my objective and subjective selves, and I have come to feel whole.

There is an archetypal power in names, and so now I name myself: I am an animist. Through the journey that has led to the integration of my disparate parts, I have come to a point of time in my life that is both very old and quite new. Old in that animism, as described by Graham Harvey in *Animism: Respecting the Living World*, refers to a belief that "the world is full of persons, only some of whom are human, and that life is always lived in relationship with others." It is a way of living in the world that made manifest good sense in the early days of human existence when each person's survival depended on both intimate knowledge about and good relations with the other-than-human world. It represented a union, or at least an integration, between objective and subjective modes of engagement with the world, exemplified by humans who recognized the "people-ness" of animals, plants, and even inanimate objects even if this recognition was, at times, directed toward killing and eating the other. Human-people share the world with deer-people, fish-people, plant-people, and even rock-people. People represent beings with which one can have a relationship, no matter that the relationship might include exchanges of matter and energy in ways that might be described as competition or predation. A true citizen of the more-than-just-human world, then, is someone who recognizes his or her ability and need to have good relationships with more beings than just humans.

Animism has been, for millennia, both a mundane and a spiritual practice for indigenous cultures on all continents, including the Americas, Europe, Asia, Africa, and Australia. Yet the practice of animism has evolved over time and has taken on aspects that are reflections of modern environmental/ecological realities. As described by religious studies scholar Graham Harvey, the focus has shifted from simply being able to identify the "person-ness" of nonhuman beings and come to include "a concern with knowing how to behave appropriately toward persons, not all of whom are human." In this modern age, which is sadly characterized by human domination of a large and increasing proportion of the structure, function, and composition of the ecosystems of the world to the detriment of humans and other-than-humans alike, learning to behave appropriately is more important than ever. Our best hope of survival may lie in recognizing that the world to which we belong extends beyond simply that made by human hands or guided by cultural rules.

My practice as an animist is grounded both in the practice

of natural history and the practice of being a good neighbor. I deliberately pay attention to the arrival and departure of birds from my neighborhood. I greet the beings in my garden, my field study sites, and all the places I travel, and I ask their permission to be there for my work or recreation. I mark the solstices and equinoxes, specifically reflecting on what that time of the year means for all of my neighbors. I make an effort, as much as I can, to acknowledge other species as people, such that in my daily life I acknowledge my interactions with bird-people, tree-people, and human-people. I make it a priority to eat food that is locally produced, and I am mindful of the relationships among beings—pollinators, decomposers, predators, producers—that make the food available to me. And I give thanks to all of my neighbors almost daily for the beauty, mystery, and community that together we create and in which together we live.

Such a practice requires mindfulness and humility in the presence of the other-than-human world. In a culture filled with so many distractions that seek to pull us *away* from the natural world, *away* from our neighbors, mindfulness can be hard to maintain. Certainly, habits and passions that take one outside frequently, even daily, help. For me, these habits are birding, gardening, and hiking. But my practice goes further, including regular conversation with my other-than-human neighbors, decorating my yard and home with symbols of their presence (the centerpoint in my garden is an ironwood post hung with antlers and mammal skulls, and my shelves throughout my home are thick with bird feathers, leaves, and shells), and decorating my skin with tattoo representations of plants and animals (for example, the Tree of Life and the Rainbow Serpent, both prominent on my right arm, where I can see them every day). Through these practices, I remain mindful of my connections, as well as the commitments I have made to remain in right relationship with the natural world even as I seek to find answers to questions about how the ecological world works.

And thus after so many years, I find that my animistic practice has brought me to a place in my journey that looks remarkably similar to the place where I began when I was twelve years old: gaining familiarity with and respecting the natural world simply because I want to know my neighbors—*all* my neighbors. Some might call this awareness "practicing natural history," but I think that too conveniently separates it from what we expect in our relationships with other humans and reinforces the unfortunate distinction between human-human and human-nature interactions. It's all people-people interactions, regardless of whether or not the people are human. It is my responsibility to learn who the people in my neighborhood are, what they do, what they need, and how my actions must be modified to take their needs into account.

It is empowering, it is rewarding, and, quite simply, it is what good neighbors do. I engage purposefully with the more-than-human world because that is what is required of someone to truly be a good neighbor. And in return, I feel connected to a larger community, a community more diverse than any made solely of humans. This connection comes with a mindful awareness of what is going on around me, and a comfort that comes with that awareness.

Long Silent Affair

Not until they could find a viable relationship to
the terrain—the physical landscape they found
themselves in—could they emerge.

—LESLIE MARMON SILKO

Cross the Rio Grande, go up a remote canyon, pass the bighorn
sheep balancing between cliffs and sky, crawl through the endless horizon, and you will come to a small village on top of a
mesa. It is here in the sweeping grandiosity, rugged wind, rough
folks, and fifty-mile views that I summoned the courage to post
a little handwritten sign on the local post office bulletin board:
"Looking to BUY or RENT a house/land—Off-grid, green-built,
unfinished OK." Within two days, the phone rang. The man on
the other end had a voice I thought I recognized as he told me
his name was Leo. He said he had a six-acre piece of land with
an unfinished straw-bale and adobe house. He told me about
hundred-year-old oak flooring and, later, the story of every fix-
ture, beam, clay plaster, and stone slab. This house was a place
of origins, a collage of Leo's love of old, beautiful things, but
also in shambles, as was his life, which is why he needed to sell
the place. I sat on a piece of his hand-built furniture, a cabinet
called a "dry-sink" painted turquoise with milk paint he had

also made by hand, and gulped, asking the price. He said three words. I knew the house was mine.

Around Taos, New Mexico, everyone knows what you mean when you say you live *on the mesa*. People just call it "The Mesa," as in classified ads reading: "Looking to rent a secluded, rural home with room for horses and my three dogs—*not* on the mesa." Or when people say to you, "Oh, god, you live on the mesa, I'm so sorry!" Or when a woman at the local store recently commented that I looked so together and refreshing, asking if I were local, because I just don't *look* like I live on the mesa . . . I like places with tough stigmas, something about being able to thrive in what others consider inhospitable or unpalatably remote. I read the morning news in the visible breaths of a hundred elk munching tall grasses in crystalline morning. Now that I've seen walls of furious water and hungry mud swallow a small pickup truck, I plan my days according to the weather. Coyote is the town crier.

I hadn't heard *all* the rumors about the mesa before I moved here, and I'm glad I didn't, because there is a secret inside the life out here, and I might have missed it. None of what you hear involves the majesty of what's really out here, and I have to wonder if this place keeps its secrets hidden behind veils of winds and furious weathers on purpose.

The word *mesa* means "table" in Spanish, Portuguese, Arabic, and the extinct language Arwi. The continents on which these languages are/were spoken all have these tablelike land formations. Since a mesa can be defined as a distinct elevated area of land with a flat top and sides, the "mesa" on which I live is actually not a mesa at all, but part of a larger geographical area known as the Taos Plateau. This plateau occurs at the southernmost part of an even larger geographical area—the sweeping,

150-mile long San Luis Basin. Taos Plateau is geologically and physiographically unique from the rest of the basin, as it is a volcanic "bench" composed almost completely of locally erupted basalts. Much of the 3- to 5-million-year-old basalt that makes up this bench, what the locals here call "the mesa," spewed forth in incandescent flows from the Tres Orejas Mountains, or "Three Peaks," which rise like soft old breasts behind my house.

I live on the flanks of ancient time.

I had no way to gauge the level of my sanity in my first days alone in this broad uplifted land above the gorged-out banks of the Rio Grande. It was August and deadeningly hot, and there wasn't a corner of my new ramshackle house that didn't need to be overhauled. When the afternoon thunderstorms would roll across the mesa with furious abandon, I was never sure whether the house would still be left standing once they passed. It rained in the kitchen, the bedroom, and the office. I would wake with a start in the night when the spotlight moon came over the rise and pierced the absolute blackness. Everyone told me a woman alone out here needs a gun, or dogs, or both. I wanted neither.

It is just past dawn. The unending light is already bearing down—the crystalline light of desert sun without a thread of water in the atmosphere. Soul-piercing light. I have just woken from a potent dream—an old friend (a man I had once spent a season in the slickrock desert with) and I have almost found each other again across the great distances fogged in by time and circumstance. He's so close in the dream I know where his foot will fall next, in rhythm with my own walking, without breaking rock or leaving a track as we move swiftly together across folds of white sandstone. I don't get to see his face even once before I wake. The already rising heat of the day sends me down through the canyon and into a thicketed-in valley of river-bottom trees, meandering like a snake across damp ground, thinking about the dream.

This man and I have seen each other exactly two times in the last seven years. I have now returned to the raw open land where our connection first took root on wind and chance alone. I am realizing now, though we've never been lovers in the conventional way, that we are entwined all the same: a flow of river through bedrock, an elusive wisp of cloud on sky.

I cross a fence and keep traveling farther into this river passageway. I don't pay heed to the trespass—isn't that what our love has always been, a forbidden place? Skirting a large *cerro*, or hill, I find a sandstone bowl around its backside, a place of fallen boulders seduced by the clinging arms of sinuous willows, a resting place for winds, and an easy place for animals to sleep in the shaded nooks of quieted time. I follow the fresh tracks of last night's coyotes moving in swift, calculated fluidity, tracking the path of the river, snaking through thickets of cottonwood, milkweed, and dogbane.

Half an hour into my wandering something draws my attention upward. There in the distance is what looks like a perfect cave fifty feet up the sandstone cliff. I look closer. Ancient footholds are worn into the stone face leading up the cliff wall to the cave. My urge is to use them, dust them out. Inside, the roof of the tiny alcove is fire-blackened. Deep vertical fissures about two feet long are worn into each of the side walls of the cave, as if someone were grinding stones into wheels, or sharpening some long item—a hundred thousand times running that same line through the soft sandstone grain. How can you not ask, "What were they doing?"

The man from my dream, I think to myself, would know the answer. And he would know it is not for the sake of antiq-

uity that I am curious, but because I have become somewhat
obsessed with survival. I imagine what this day would be like if
there were no society as we know it going on over the hills from
here: Would I be sitting here making pots from stream-bank
clay, to be fired in the cave above?

Then a clap of thunder speaks just one word, and I get the
immediate jolt that I am not alone out there in the canyon. The
palpable weight of presences comes in on a warm wind.

I have been too much indoors—this spooks me more than I
would have wanted it to.

I climb down the inlaid ladder and sit with my back against
warm stone. Now I am listening to the voice of the sand to try
to find the man from my dream in it, I have my arms spread
toward the top of the windy canyon, beckoning ravens to take
my message to wherever he might be. I am kneeling in front of
the river and making gifts, little leaf-boats full of prayers that
get whooshed down into spirals of furious water.

Above and to the side of the cave there is another ladder,
a shallowly inlaid set of steps and tricky handholds set in the
sandstone leading to a tiny room, perhaps a cache of some sort,
almost impossible to see or get to—but friend, you're teaching
me how to read this old landscape. Everywhere, you are right,
there are routes. But my body forgets how to move up them.
And perhaps I'm not allowed in there anyway. What makes us
think, just because we find a treasure, that it is ours to collect?

This is what we are up against: Everything can be violated.
But sometimes we have the sense not to violate. I withdraw my
hand from the temptation of touching the first dusty handhold
of the upper ladder and leave the cache unmarred.

Then there was a trail of bones flowing down in an old path
of water. And in one of the in-dug footholds down the crum-
bling sandstone, an owl pellet, the upturned stomach of a bird

who eats the flesh and spits out the bones. Having left the other cache undisturbed, I am compelled to dig through this one, a scavenger for what no one else finds valuable. I mine three perfect leg bones out of the scat, each an inch long, not an eighth of an inch thick. I want to gamble with them, but I don't know the old bone games. If I could, I would roll these kangaroo rat bones and divine the summer weather, determine the timing of my next moves . . . Instead I take them home, back through the canyon and up the mesa, and put them on the sill of the window to be read by night wind passing over them where they lay tossed in a random pattern next to where I sleep.

How long will I love this place in solitude?

I have conversations with essences and daydreams, someone who may be hearing some hint on the wind of what I am saying. I live here for the quiet, but I am not naive about the fact that the quiet has the capacity to undo me.

I want to believe in the power of the words we speak only in the inconceivably lonely places, interior and exterior.

Is it too erotic to ask: *Do you know what it feels like to sit naked, open to the flowing river, coursing water catapulting through bare body, bare bedrock?* And if so, why do I have to experience intimacy only with place itself, which does not blush, but opens to my pleas and incessant inquiries? But isn't human love infinitely more complex? This long silent affair with canyons and flowing waters, winds and unending sky would surely be eclipsed by the laughter and struggle of companionship. And so I realize I *am* happy in this conversation after all. River, sand, bones, longing, every syllable draws me further toward this elusive conversation, toward replacing my understanding of loneliness with only *this* kiss—solitude in contact with the wild now.

Then I look down with a more careful eye, and beyond the cryptogamic soil, beyond the broken pieces of cholla laid spiny and bare on open rock, is a pocket of mica-infused clay, inundated by water. I am compelled to touch it. Two minutes out of the water the clay begins to solidify. This is a pot. This is pot shards. This is the prayer that is the smoothing of the inside of the wet body of the pot as it is being made. This is the lovemaking before we've even met.

Then I know what I have to do. Put the clay back into the water. Dream on it a little longer. Travel up the mesa in the sharp sun and leave this canyon to the coyotes and its ancient inhabitants.

What I want to know is this: If I come back and make something with this clay, can I go as far back into any canyon as I have ever been? Can I climb into the snaking folds of calcified time to find a ledge where I may secretly leave this pot as the ancient gift of now? Which trespasses feed the world, and which destroy it?

Back on the mesa the canyon below is a far-away rivulet like a furrow seen from an airplane. The tiny bones rest on the stone-slab window ledge above my bed. I occupy territory in this land like those who dwelled in the canyons long ago: belonging to the moods of the winds, the intensities of light, the long exhales of passing seasons. I am lured on by the patterns of bones and tracks, by dreams and silence-induced visions, by the interplay between the sacred ancient past and the possibility of that relationship in the present.

Bear Sign (On Joyous Attention)

To get to our cabin from the cove where we moor our boat, we walk a trail known as Bear Alley. The trail cuts through head-high grasses and enters a damp tunnel of alders and hemlocks. This is the same path the brown bears follow to move from the abundance of sedge on the beach to the skunk cabbage in the dark stream that feeds the cove. Another path cuts away from the cove and follows the streambed into the mountain meadows. Bears have used this path for so many hundreds of years that they have worn it into a narrow, flat-bottomed ditch—a foot wide, maybe, a foot deep in the duff and moss, winding up the mountainside through lady ferns and Sitka spruce.

Our cabin sits in a blueberry thicket at the place where the stream enters the sea, which is to say, at the place where the bear trail that descends the mountain meets the bear trail that circles the cove. There are many more bears than people on this Alaskan island, and at least a couple of bears follow these paths each day. From my bunk at the window in the cabin, I often wake to see a bear grazing in the cove, big and calm as a cow.

Am I afraid of the bears? Yes, in fact, I am. These are Alaskan

brown bears, seacoast grizzlies grown huge and sleek on
salmon. I want to live my allotted time, not find myself prema-
turely swatted into eternity because I got myself in the way of
a bear. It doesn't matter that never, in the memory of this inlet,
has anyone been so much as bruised by a bear; when I walk
up the trail (usually carrying a five-gallon bucket of halibut or
crabs) or walk down the trail (usually carrying a bucket of fish
carcasses or crab shells), I am sharply attentive.

That circle of beaten-down grass—how long ago did a bear
bed down there? That pile of bear scat like Ping-Pong balls
woven of sedge—has that been here since spring, when bears
headed from their dens to the beach for a first meal? That patch
of ground pines popping out of the duff—bears love them. If a
bear had passed recently, wouldn't all the ground pines be bit-
ten off at the stems? Have hemlock needles fallen on that pile of
scat? Has rain softened the edges of the paw-print in the mud?
I stop to examine the bear scratching-post at the intersection of
the trails. The bark on the tree is rubbed to a fine polish. I look
for new patches of grizzled fur stuck in the cracks.

I scan the forest constantly, alert for a brown hump in the
salmonberries. I listen, turning my head. Disturbed bears don't
growl. They huff. Quiet as the huffing is—as easily mistaken for
water against stones—when it comes from behind a screen of
alder trees, this is a sound that catches one's attention. Sometimes if I'm approaching a rise or a dense patch of berries, I'll let
out a *hoo-eee*, as if I were calling pigs. But most of the time on
the trail, I sing. I sing the songs my mother taught me, whatever
old campfire song comes to mind. So it's *I love to go a-wandering
along the mountain track, and as I go I love to sing, my knapsack
on my back* that causes a bear to lift its head, look long in my
direction, then with unmistakable dignity stroll off on a course
diagonally away from mine, as if that was the way the bear

wanted to go all along. *Valderi, valdera, valderi, valdera-hahaha haha valderi, valdera, my knapsack on my back.*

I have decided this is not a bad way to walk in the woods—with this kind of attention, with this singing.

If my father had lived long enough to join us here in the wilderness, he would be on his knees, poking a stick into a bear pile, sorting out a beetle's wing or identifying the genus and species of the undigested grass. My father was the person who taught me to pay attention. He was a naturalist for the Rocky River parks when my sisters and I were small. His job was to lead field trips on Sunday mornings along the river or into the beech-maple forest under the approach path for Cleveland Hopkins airport. Each Saturday before a field trip, he would load up the family, and off we would go. My sisters and I were the designated Finders of Interesting Things. We lifted sheets of bark off fallen logs to find slick black salamanders, and turned stones along the river looking for dragonfly larvae. I remember finding a hummingbird's nest made of lichen and spiderwebs, tiny as an eggcup. If we found a plant we couldn't identify, we called my father over and he keyed it out, step by step. Jewelweed, he would say. Squeeze the seedpod just this way to see it pop. We sang along with birdcalls. *Old Sam Peabody Peabody Peabody*: the white-throated sparrow. We poked sticks down crayfish mud-towers and tried to find fossils in the shale. In cups folded from mayapple leaves, we carried water striders into a puddle to watch them fight.

By the next day, my father had become a magician. With his pet raccoon on his shoulder, he led a string of people who had skipped church for a "nature walk." Look here, he would say, you can often find salamanders under fallen logs. And there it would be—skinny, shiny, glorious. Can you find a bird's nest in this fir?

he would ask, and someone did—and not just any bird nest, but a hummingbird nest made of lichen and spiderwebs. He knew every birdcall, knew the name of every plant—in Latin and in English. He knew why only female mosquitoes bite. He knew why stinging nettles sting. It didn't matter that airliners regularly roared over the tops of the trees or that teenagers washed their Thunderbirds in the river upstream. For the people on the field trip, the morning was a great satisfaction. They found what they were looking for, which, as I think about it now, must have been an intimacy with the everyday marvelous, the miracle you can cup in your hand.

If my mother were here walking the bear trails, she would be organizing us to sing rounds. You start, you're second, you come in third, she would say. If we are going to sing to alert the bears to our presence, we will give them a rousing chorus, not insult them with a single line of song. It is harmony, after all, that we seek, harmony that will save us. *All things shall perish from under the sky. Music alone shall live, never to die.* If my mother were here, we would march across the mudflat, keeping one eye on the bear on the far side of the cove, making harmony the way a round makes harmony, weaving the song like sedge is woven in bear droppings in the spring, pausing to hold an especially beautiful chord as a gift to the bears. My mother taught us dozens of rounds, and so we learned to listen, to be attentive to the music of others, to tune ourselves to their chords, to pace ourselves to their rhythms. We learned that weaving songs is one of the most beautiful things we can do, and we can't do it by ourselves.

My mother was a Girl Scout when she was young, just come to America, and that's where she learned the old stories and the campfire songs about wild places. *It's the far northland that's a-calling me away.* Or, *If there were witchcraft, I'd make three wishes. A winding road that beckons me to roam.* I don't think her scout troop ever went to the far northland or followed the winding road; I wonder now if that made her sad, or if it was enough to sing about *seeing the loon and hearing its plaintive wail.* That was before she went off to World War II to help rehabilitate soldiers. She was the nurse who led the singing therapies. I can imagine all the grievously wounded soldiers, pale on white sheets, singing *I love to go a-wandering, along the mountain track.* And maybe that was healing. Maybe that was exactly what they needed, to sing in harmony from all the beds in the ward, to sing in harmony from the place of their lonely grief, the song of the Happy Wanderer.

Can it save our lives, this joyous attention?

In a literal sense, it might someday. Pay attention, and you might see a bear before it sees you. Then you can stop, group up with your friends, and find another way to go, even if it means crashing through the devil's club that stings the backs of your hands. Sing, and the bear will hear you coming even if the creek is in her ears. Then maybe she will remember she has an appointment in another place.

So joyous attention might save someone in that small way. But there's much more to it than that. Thomas Berry wrote, "We are most ourselves when we are most intimate with the rivers and the mountains and woodlands, with the sun and the moon and the stars in the heavens; when we are most intimate with the air we breathe, the Earth that supports us, . . . with the meadows in bloom. . . . However we think of eternity, it can only be an aspect of the present."

Some cultures might find intimacy in ritual or prayer, in dance and art, in food or drink. But it seems to me that in our very peculiar Western culture, we find intimacy through understanding. Afraid of mystery, we want to know about things—

how they work, how they're put together, what their names are, and how they are related. Knowledge delights us. The more we learn, the more clearly we understand the density of the webs that connect one thing to another, and humankind to it all. Each of us is so much more than we think we are—these hands, this body, these sorrows and hopes. We are air exhaled by hemlocks, we are water plowed by whales, we are matter born in stars, we are children of deep time. How can we be fully alive if we don't pause to notice—and to celebrate—the full extension of our being into time and the universe?

Here on the island, our family takes great trouble to protect the full *length* of our lives. The first thing visitors notice is the bear spray in the outhouse. The second is the shotgun on the shelf above the cabin door. What if we put as much energy into extending the *depth* of each moment we live? I think this is what joyous attention can do: to attend to the layers of time embedded in the boulder on the beach, to notice the successive years in a spruce stump splintered by the splitting maul. In every way, to celebrate what links a person and a place—love, of course, and origins, sustenance and fate. There are natural limits to the length of a person's life, but the meaning of a moment is infinitely deep. In exploring the connected webs of meaning, we come as close to eternity as we will ever be.

In the path in front of our cabin, there is a place where bears record their presence on the Earth. What you see there looks like eight indentations in the trail—right paw, left paw, right—as if a Paul Bunyan bear had hammered his paw-prints into the dirt as he strode by. We are told that this is exactly what it is. Year after year, bears scuff their paw-prints in the soft soil, placing their paws in exactly the same places each time. With depressions in the soil, they make a record of their passing.

Our friends and I tried this, leaning down to put our hands in the forepaw prints, stretching our legs to reach the prints of the hind paws, and then lumbering along, butt in the air, nose to the ground like the world's most inadequate bear. Finally, we tipped onto the ground in our yellow raincoats, laughing and afraid, humbled by the paw-prints of a bear. This might be a good place for a human to be, this close to the earth—smelling, as the bear smells, the sweetness of skunk cabbage, the seaweed-salt of intertidal flats, the melted-snow sharpness of air off the mountain; knowing, the way the bear knows, the rolling of the seasons; living, the way the bear lives, the sharply attentive life, layered with danger and possibility; glad for whatever taste of eternity is open to us, which is not to live forever, but to live in the deep meaning of each moment of our allotted time.

Yard Birds

Like a bird on the wire
like a drunk in a midnight choir
I have tried in my way to be free.

—LEONARD COHEN, *"Bird on a Wire"*

Now, the real heat begins: the dry, lip-splitting, nose-blistering, ear-ringing heat of foresummer. We reached 100 degrees Fahrenheit at 1:58 p.m. today, which is on schedule for the end of May in the Sonoran Desert. As sunlight talcums the landscape, shadows are reduced to thin anemic lines on the ground. Like me, shadows become territorial, slipping beneath their stones at noon and emerging late in the day to venture out tentatively across the prison yard. Shadows can never go too far.

As if to celebrate the climatic benchmark, the cicadas have begun to sing. Theirs is the quintessential sound of summer, of the energy held in the coming monsoon thunderstorms, concentrated into a squat gray insect and unloaded when the desert is empty of everything except faith.

With the heat comes both an absence and presence of birds. I have just learned to see warblers, and now they are gone. But the season's first turkey vultures have returned from their southward migration last fall, and I'm expecting lesser night-hawks, members of the weak-footed, dirt-sitting clan called goatsuckers, which should be arriving from Mexico soon to nest on our abundant bare ground outside the perimeter fence, feeding after dark on insects drawn to the security lights.

I go looking for nighthawks as the sun touches the hori-zon, casting its longer, redder wavelengths into a reef of clouds. Mourning doves turn my head as they cross the sky on their way to find overnight roosts. It's still too early. On my third circuit of the prison yard I think I see boomerang wings and the languid maneuvering of a nighthawk, but the bird is too far away. On my next lap I'm certain one drifts by Housing Unit Two, sculling through bug-rich cones of light. I need to get closer. Before I'm ready to return to my cell, another one glides past, this one directly in front of me. Three nighthawks in less than an hour, but the birds still seem ephemeral, theoretical.

This changes more than a month later, following a monsoon thunderstorm with its windstain of wet creosote. In the eve-ning's post-storm quiet, crunching over washed gravel on my way back to my cell, I notice a low-flying nighthawk circling the area between Dorm Four and Housing Unit Two. The bird continues to dip between the buildings as I approach and cross into its airspace. It feeds on winged insects, protean clouds that vibrate in the air. I sit on the concrete steps to watch and discover a termite hatch. As if gravity were unwinding, silken chutes spray out of the bare ground directly to my left.

The nighthawk is insatiable. For fifteen minutes I trail the owl-like bird with my eyes as it sifts the air with its wide-mouthed, whiskered beak. I'm participating in something intimate, silent yet potent: termite nuptials and nighthawk gluttony; the ecstasy of consummation and consumption.

There's something about being able to *see* in this place, to measure the dimensions of prison so clearly. But there are also days when I don't get it right, when my sight is dimmed, like the time a cactus wren chattered from a loop of razor wire next to East Gate. The cactus wren is our state bird, and I couldn't help but think, *How appropriate—this bird on a wire*. What I record in my journal for that day is a rant: "The scene should be on Arizona's state seal," I write. "*Ditat Deus Incarceratamus*: God enriches, we incarcerate."

And I can't seem to stop there:

> The Great Seal of the State of Arizona features mountains and sunset, valley farmland, a cow, a miner with a shovel (or is it a convict with a shovel?)—all symbols relating to the once-important economic activities of mining, ranching, and agriculture. The three C's: copper, cattle, and cotton. Since the decline of these industries, and the curious subsequent boom in crime legislation, prisons have become the ore and livestock and crops to stimulate the economies of played-out mining towns like Douglas and Globe, and dustbowl farming towns like Florence, Yuma, Safford, Perryville, Buckeye, and Picacho. Altogether, more than fifty prison units in ten major complexes crisscross Arizona, creating ten thousand jobs and making the Arizona Department of Corrections one of the largest employers in the state. Arizona should revise its state seal of 1912. It's outdated. Today the three C's really mean crime, convicts, and corrections.

How is it that I couldn't see the wren for all the razor wire? If I fail to pay attention, my reality could easily erase the wonderful, particularly because my reality has Orwellian overtones. But isn't wilderness here as much a reality as prison walls? Even here, nature penetrates. The birds, the insects, the weather, the impenitent weeds—all trespass this fenced human landfill. If I am not going to accept prison as only a time of confinement, I have to strive to constantly cobble nature onto concrete and steel, focusing on the transgressions of wildness in whatever form they take. I can't allow prison to form a patina over my view of the world or I will find it impossible to reenter the world and see the wonder of the simplest things, like ratchet-voiced cactus wrens bright in the sun. It's not so much what you look at but what you see.

I make dark laps around the prison yard this quiet, hot evening. The moon turns away from the horizon as if snubbed, and I walk a course along my northern perimeter and its frayed hem of chain-link and razor wire. Suddenly, something out of place catches my eye. A brown pelican traces the fence. The bird is huge, prehistoric, reptilian, with bent wings that lean into a Cretaceous sky as it drifts, circles, and slips out of view. It could be my imagination, this web-footed, gular-pouched misfit hunting surf perch in the desert sand. But it's real.

Here, in a place that scours you down to the essences of appetite and hope, the moon and stars are my bread and water. Sprays of termites, nighthawk ballets, and even an abandoned pelican feather holding a slip of sky against its vane are the air that fills my lungs.

Maintenance

Our friend Gillian Coote of Sydney, Australia, takes part in a program called Bush Regeneration. She and her friends work a space of public, neglected land, pull all the weeds and remove plants and trees that are not native—then move on to the next block. Seeds of native plants can freely sprout and flourish in the cleared land, and gradually Australia becomes itself once again.

Without Bush Regeneration or a similar program of maintenance, the land becomes as alien as its exotic invaders. Naturalists in the state administration of Hawai'i are keenly aware of this danger and campaign against a South American interloper, *Micronia calvescens*, that can smother native plants and their habitat. It has been a reasonably successful campaign here, but not so in Tahiti. I remember seeing a rural valley there twenty-five years ago that was awash in micronia. High on a ridge I could see a lone tree fern, almost completely swamped, struggling to lift a frond.

Maybe the Tahitian authorities are looking for an insect from elsewhere that will eat the micronia for them. There is plenty of precedent for this expedient, but all too often the insect or animal that solves the immediate difficulty turns out to be another enemy. Alien birds, animals, and insects introduced accidentally or on misguided purpose have produced problems—not just in Pacific islands, but in specific areas across the world—the subject of rueful jokes everywhere about noxious toads, singing frogs, mynah birds, and mongooses.

There are human social analogies as well. Earnest missionaries from foreign lands have effected the entire destruction of cultures and their peoples. It is no exaggeration to say that the United States has been intent with lethal weaponry to prove that the only good Muslim either is no longer Muslim or is dead, together with whole cities and farming communities and Muslim culture itself.

The practice of the noble must be informed and assiduous care for the unique and therefore precious beings of the world. "However innumerable beings may be, I vow to have them cross over to Nirvana"—so we as Zen Buddhists recite each day in wording that varies from center to center. I vow to make it possible for them to reach their own maturity, in other words. These beings range from our solar system, which surely will eventually respond negatively to garbage in space, to microscopic creatures that also have roles in the vast living network of all existence, but can kick back viciously if they are misused.

Our vow is global and involves a clear sense of proportion. Just because the micronia appears in my backyard here in Honolulu doesn't mean that I should make it possible for it to reach maturity. "Sorry, pretty plant, you don't belong here!" *Chop!*

The cockroach has its cleanup function outdoors, but in the baby's crib, *swat!* "Better luck next time!" I remember how Anne Aitken would catch a cockroach in a jar and turn it loose outside with the farewell, "Be happy!"

I also remember catching a big rat in a Havahart trap in our kitchen here at Pālolo. I walked her up the road in her trap and released her into the bushes. She scooted off, and just before disappearing she turned and looked back at me. "We're all in it together," I read into that look.

The vow to enhance the lives of all beings is the practice of maintaining in context. The context of the mother is the health of her baby, who is endangered by the filthy feet of the cockroach. The context of the rat is her babies back in her nest. The context of the Muslim is his heritage, society, and deeply imprinted religious training.

The context of zazen is thoughts that rise endlessly. Here is a story I've told before:

> Guishan Lingyu asked Lazy An, "How do you practice all day long?"
> Lazy An said, "I tend an ox."
> Guishan asked, "How do you tend it?"
> Lazy An said, "Whenever it strays into the grass, I pull it back by the nose."
> Guishan said, "You are truly tending that ox."

The context of the ox is fresh rich grass, but it is alien weed, and isn't true food. Your context is lovely thoughts of jackpot or seduction, but they get in the way. Pull yourself back by the nose! That is maintenance! That is practice!

Ordinary thoughts of wealth and sex are not the only distractions. Teachings and their interpretation can also lead us astray. Bassui Tokushō dismissed even astute preoccupations and sacred incantations like this:

> When analytical thoughts are forgotten, views based on knowledge are also forgotten, leaving no trace of ego. The path where heavenly beings fulfill their desire to offer flowers no longer exists. What special incantation can compare to this? It is said in a sutra, "On perceiving that the five skandhas (form, feeling, perceptions, impulses

and consciousness) are empty, one is freed from all kinds of pain and misfortune." There is no gate through which demons and heretics can secretly enter. If, while devoting yourself to practice, and thinking that it will prevent the interference from demons, you recite invocations from sutras, this kind of reasoning will create a demon inside you, attracting demons from the outside and causing chaos within, like a stinking carcass attracts blowflies.

This criticism is not condemnation—it is an exposition of the way to be human, with human responsibility to maintain the self with discipline. It is an exposition of the way to maintain the human role in the world as dominion over all—with dominion clearly defined as our First Vow—to make it possible for all beings to attain to their own fulfillment.

Here again, a clear sense of proportion is essential. "All beings" includes Iraqis and Afghans. It includes victims of Hurricane Katrina. It includes Native Americans, Native Alaskans, and Native Hawaiians. The First Vow is a pledge to invest rigorously in peace and social justice as occasions for response arise. To sit back and let "activists" invest themselves for you is to betray the clear intent of the Dharma. This is the world—our Zen practice and our context in our neighborhood, which has no bounds and extends everywhere. There is no "other world."

It is important also to acknowledge the place of ritual in maintaining ourselves and fulfilling our First Vow. All beings are invited to drop away body and mind together (that is, to root out alien stuff completely). In Zen, the ritual of doing things together is the practice of dropping away. The ceremony of accepting alms and food would be an example. It is *pindipata* in ancient Sanskrit, *tobo* in Chinese, *takuhatsu* in Japanese—the formal walk by monks in a single line through town to accept contributions. They are dressed in their oldest robes, with a special bag over their *rakusu* to receive money and rice. As they walk they sing out the syllable *hō* (expedient means), which somehow rises above the noise of traffic, and they walk with their hands held formally together just above the belt. It is a sight that brings the ancient into the most modern of contexts.

Once long ago when I was on *takuhatsu* in the town of Mishima with the monks of Ryūtakuji, a monk who had recently joined the sangha from another monastery walked with us. He walked with his arms swinging, instead of holding his hands together. Gempō Rōshi heard about the monk's conduct from a friend in town and devoted a good part of his next *teishō* to taking us all to task for the infraction. What a great lesson!

When all is said and done, our fundamental practice of maintenance is zazen. As we sit there, all things breathe together as reminders—the sound of raindrops, the bell calling all to supper, the cough of a friend, a sudden idea. As the old Hindus would say, "Neti! Neti!" (Not this! Not this!). The extraneous aliens are thus our friends, prodding us along. Bassui Zenji puts it like this:

> The mind is originally pure. It was not born with this body and does not die with its extinction. What's more, it cannot be distinguished as male or female, or shaped as good or bad. It is beyond any comparison so we call it Buddha-nature. Moreover, like waves from the ocean, the many thoughts arise out of this original nature. They are like reflections from a mirror. That's why you must first see where thoughts come from, if you want to understand your mind. So whether asleep or awake, standing or sitting, you must question deeply, "What is this mind?" The deep desire to realize this is called religious practice, training, aspiration for the Way-seeking mind. Questioning your mind in this manner is also referred to as zazen.

A Nat'ral Histerrical Feller in an Unwondering Age

One touch of Nature makes the whole world kin.

—WILLIAM SHAKESPEARE, *Troilus and Cressida*

For anyone seriously interested in North American butterflies in the first half of the twentieth century, the primary reference by a long shot was W. J. Holland's *The Butterfly Book*. Published in 1898 and revised in 1931, its final 1950s impression included my own copy. The charm and interest of Holland's big tome, hardly a field guide, were much enhanced for young readers by a series of "Digressions and Quotations." These ranged from the author's own recollections of important moments with butterflies, to verse by Hugo (translated by Eugene Field), Ella Wheeler Wilcox, and "Mrs. Hemans." Vladimir Nabokov, a stern critic of "old Dr. Holland," dismissed these marginalia as "stale anecdotes . . . and third-rate poetry." Lowbrow though they may be, these bits made the ponderous work more fun, and like many a young lepidopterist of the era, I practically memorized them through successive rainy-day readings.

One such piece, "Uncle Jotham's Boarder" by Annie Trumbull Slosson, tells in stylized dialect the story of a summer boarder at a rural farmhouse, and his perception by his host. Uncle Jotham reported his guest's activities in anthropological detail:

> Well, true as I live, that old feller just spent
> His hull days in loafin' about
> And pickin' up hoppers and roaches and flies
> Not to use for his bait to ketch trout
> But to kill and stick pins in and squint at and all.
> He was crazy's a coot, th' ain't no doubt.

When the boarder tries to explain why he feeds "ellums and birches and willers" to boxes of caterpillars in his bedroom, Uncle Jotham concludes, "S'near's I can tell, 'stead of enterin' a trade, / He was tryin' to just enter *mology*." He continues:

> And Hannah, my wife, says she's heard o' sech things;
> She guesses his brain warn't so meller.
> There's a thing they call Nat'ral Histerry, she says.
> And whatever the folks here may tell her
> Till it's settled she's wrong she'll just hold that 'air man
> Was a Nat'ral Histerrical feller.

No matter how many times I read it, I always got a giggle out of the silly pun. It also served to remind me that I, too, was a "nat'ral histerrical feller," and that not everyone else was. But the verse also reinforced a message I got loud and clear every time I went out in public with my own "old bait net": one of surprise, amusement, and, often, even derision. Most folks didn't know what to make of my passion. I lived in a 1960s suburban setting, but as Mrs. Slosson's fin de siècle rural verse suggests, country people shared that bemusement toward a naturalist in their midst with the suburbanites. For the most part, I withstood the cracks and hoots; but I've seen many other kids hang up their nets under the pressure of conformity, especially in adolescence. It helped me to know that I wasn't the only nature freak ever to be cast an incredulous eye. But it was another bit of Holland's borrowed verse that pointed me toward my life-long objective—not just to know some "nat'ral histerry," but to inquire deeply of nature. His follow-up volume, *The Moth Book*, begins with this dialogue by Oliver Wendell Holmes in *The Poet at the Breakfast Table*:

> "I suppose you are an entomologist?"
> "Not quite as ambitious as that, sir. I should like to put my eyes on the individual entitled to that name. No man can be truly called an entomologist, sir; the subject is too vast for any human intelligence to grasp."

If it was a vast challenge that Holland and Holmes hurled my way, they also served up a useful corrective to my childish conceit: After all, if it was impossible to become a real entomologist, how could one hope to embrace natural history as a whole? But as I soon learned, this particular uphill road was full of delights. I might never get there, but I would have fun trying. Ultimately, the attempt would define my life.

There was a time when most members of every social band were pretty good working naturalists, or they didn't survive. But "civilization" meant compartmentalizing jobs and functions, so that the intimate knowledge of flora and fauna possessed by the people became the province of shamans, priests, and wise women. (The first such division of labor, following the hunter/gatherer fault, may have broken along gender lines: animal-savvy men vs. plantswomen. Until relatively recent times, women in life sciences were much more likely to be found in botany departments than zoology.)

In their modern eras, most cultures have found natural history retreating into smaller and smaller crannies and obscure recesses. England seemed to be the one exception, where "countryside" pursuits remained more or less common until fairly recent times. But that was an aberration, and it has in any case faded. In general, contemporary culture has marginalized the naturalist with impressive thoroughness. After all, naturalists know what's going on out there, which gets in the way of progress.

There was also a time when professionals were trained and hired to attend to natural history for the rest of us: the systematists, curators, fieldworkers, professors, and so on. But that was Holland's time, and he was one of them, as director of the Carnegie Museum. From midcentury on, a purge of the naturalists occurred at many universities, in favor of molecular, cellular, and mathematical biology. The University of Washington conducted its final entomological field trip this past summer, after a century of insect instruction. Great museums went increasingly for big exhibits over basic study, neglecting their vital collections. Even as professional, academic natural history went into eclipse, the regular presence of outdoor subjects in the public schools (inspired by Anna Botsford Comstock's nature-study movement) withered to near nothingness, capped off by Sputnik. Environmental education has never managed to replace nature study, whereby a basic working knowledge of local fauna and flora was considered an essential part of education.

Now that we've come to a time when understanding all the working parts of the biosphere is more important than ever, the number of people charged with and compensated for doing so is smaller than ever. Most detailed biological survey and systematic study is now performed by amateurs who do it for love, as the term implies, in concert with a handful of hold-out pros at the Smithsonian, the McGuire Center for Biological Diversity in Gainesville, and a few other overstretched institutions. One elder woman and her son possess most of the knowledge of West

Coast worms. A volunteer devout is the primary authority on spiders of the Pacific Northwest. The greatest North American butterfly taxonomist is a swing-shift truck driver. They are not unusual. As Carol Kaesuk Yoon puts it in *Naming Nature: The Clash between Instinct and Science,* "We are willfully . . . losing the ability to order and name and therefore losing a connection to and a place in the living world."

Oddly enough, despite such trends, natural history has bounced back in the United States in some ways. Television and Internet features and series, bird-watching and feeding, butter-flying, native plants and gardening groups are all popular and growing. The drive toward green has made nature fashionable again. But most of this attention is shallow. People too often ignore what they separate from themselves as "nature," and of those members who do notice or even celebrate it, few explore the real, living, more-than-human world in any depth. It's better than nothing, is about all you can say.

If Americans on the whole are profoundly ignorant about natural history, and they are, then most of the "naturalists" among them aren't much better. Most birders don't know their local flora. The majority of butterfly watchers of my acquaintance have little knowledge of other orders of insects, let alone other groups of invertebrates. Gardeners often have little sense of plant families, knowing nothing of the relatives and progenitors of their favorite flowers or veggies. Few modern hunters and fishers know many non-game species by name or habit. And children, the original naturalists, recognize many more corporate logos today than animals or plants, as recent studies have shown. Some enthusiasts cross over, such as bird-watchers who discover butterflies as a new challenge, jokingly known as "birders gone bad." The equivalent for butterfly watchers is to take up dragonfly-watching. But the majority of nature lovers tend to stick to familiar territory.

Last year, I traveled over much of the United States conducting the first Butterfly Big Year. One of my hopes was to conduct a broad overview of butterfly well-being. Aside from general development, the single factor most often cited for local or regional extirpation of rare butterflies was fire, wild or intentional. The lack of baseline data for pre-burn, fire-intolerant butterflies allows fires to go ahead with no awareness of their consequences—the pyrobotanists literally know not what they do. The Ottoe skipper has been wiped out of Iowa and much of the Midwest, largely by controlled burns—too hot, too big, too often—on state and private reserves. And that's just butterflies! What about the many more moths? The flies, wasps, and other pollinators? Let alone the cities of soil invertebrates. In fact, there is usually no one available to identify invertebrates, even if managers *did* attempt due diligence in baseline sampling.

Our culture neither values nor rewards, let alone trains and hires, well-versed naturalists. Is it any wonder that we are a nation (and a world) of natural history ignoramuses? Our ecological illiteracy achieves a scale no less than spectacular. Most nature writers, poets of the more-than-human, environmental studies professionals, landscape engineers and planners, and others whom we might expect to know better actually have very little natural history at their disposal. Among the worst are some of the so-called, self-described "deep ecologists," ecopsychologists, and spiritual ecophilosophers.

In my experience, though nice enough folks with admirable ethics and intentions, many such people don't know squat about actual ecosystems. Next time you meet a "deep ecologist," ask him to explain the trophic levels in his backyard, complete with plot and cast. On your next walk with a person with eco-anything on her business card, ask for an introduction to the local flora and fauna. Some may be able to accommodate—but most? I am not putting down these people, practices, or professions, but their self-awarded titles often strike me as ironic, if not hubristic.

The plain fact is, there are very few deep naturalists, as I would define the term: someone with a working knowledge of a broad slice of the biota, and how the parts fit together with one another and their physical setting. After fifty-plus years of hanging about with thousands of biologists and nature lovers, I can think of just a handful who even come close: Dennis Paulson in Seattle, Joe Alcock in Phoenix, Roger Hammer down in Homestead, Bill Leonard up in Olympia come to mind: humble aspirants all, who would probably not accept the title I am giving them. I'm sure there are many others I don't know. But serious practitioners of the principles Ann Zwinger exemplifies in her splendid book *The Nearsighted Naturalist* are, by any measure, few.

Lately, programs have arisen to certify naturalists, along the lines of Master Gardeners. It's a nice idea, designed to increase people's confidence in teaching others. But no one knows enough to even ask the test questions. I have always said that anyone out of doors with open eyes (and/or ears) and mind is a naturalist, and I believe it. That lets most folks out, right there. But a deep naturalist (let alone a Master Naturalist—ha!) would have a passable knowledge of many groups of organisms, their lifeways, and the processes that bind them together, as well as geology, climatology, and much more. Do you know many such? Any?

I do know many experts on given groups of organisms. Perhaps it is asking too much of anyone to know a lot of groups, habitats, and phenomena, like asking Joshua Bell to also be Dr. John and Merle Haggard. But what's to keep one from trying to know something of everything out there? Perhaps what we need is a better class of dilettantes.

At this point, I should make it very clear that I consider myself a dilettante when it comes to most aspects of natural history, if not an outright ignoramus. People think I know a lot about nature, but I snort at that. Perhaps I do, compared to most, but that only reinforces my depressing point. I know "a lot" about butterflies, but far less than fifty or one hundred people I could immediately name, and a great many more I don't know. And though I know my local birds, plants, mammals, mollusks, herps, some moths, fish, and a few others, I know very little about our magnificent fly fauna, our lichens, or the water bears that surely clamber through our anonymous, sopping mosses in winter. No one else does, either. How dispiriting! That flying termite at my feet, that moth, that midge . . . who are *they*? I thirst to know them all—not just their names, but something of their lives.

It would be unreasonable to expect many people to seek a really deep knowledge of natural history. The sheer quantity of ecological information is daunting, to be sure. Besides, the banal details of quotidian life won't allow it, with most of us who are "caught between the longing for love and the struggle for the legal tender," as Jackson Browne so perfectly put it. The stupidifying effects of contemporary culture take care of the rest of the possibility for many, by miring their spare time in trivia. But in a culture that hopes to stick around for a while, is it too much to ask its members to get to know a few of their nonhuman neighbors? A bird a week, a plant a month, a beetle a year—it's not that hard.

For my part, I aspire someday toward the middle rungs of

deep natural history. But this is no competition. In my Butterfly Big Year, I attended to every other group I noticed as well, to some extent. With the help of field guides, book and human, I noted around a thousand distinct animal species (though I didn't have a name for every one) along with countless plants. This was satisfying, and put again a question I've often asked: How do people survive *sans* natural history? The nature I know has saved my life, over and over. It also lets me know how much I don't know, and causes me to crave a deeper immersion than I've known so far. We can never know it all, but there's nothing to keep us from becoming better acquainted with our surroundings, a little bit every day.

I used to imagine an island—I knew one or two that would nicely suffice—on which I would camp and try to get to know every single occupant over the years. But islands are hard to come by, difficult of access and supply, and lack certain elements, thanks to island biogeography. Now I live on a kind of an island—a little three-acre pie-slice of land between two roads and a creek. It is an old Swedish homestead, known as Swede Park, in the southwestern Washington rainforest. I told its story in *Sky Time in Gray's River: Living for Keeps in a Forgotten Place*. People think I know its natural history in depth, but I laugh. I would love to. And maybe I will make the attempt.

I am sixty-two—with luck, I've got maybe thirty or forty years left. What to do with it? More and more, natural history is what makes sense to me. I have fought many conservation battles, and will continue to do so, as quixotic as it often seems. But I have grown anaphylactically allergic to committees and almost all meetings. I have lost most interest in distant cities. I gave up TV in 1969, and the Internet, largely, forty years later. I spend much of my time perforce before a screen in order to write, and I just don't feel the need to entertain myself in the same posture.

Without a doubt, the Internet offers vastly greater information about natural history, and closer communication among
naturalists. The superb www.butterfliesofamerica.org is just
one example. However, I've watched many colleagues dissipate
much of their available time and energy in ephemeral e-mail
fusillades and repetitive, unrefereed disputation. I will surely
use the Internet for specific information search and concise
communication, but I refuse to devote to it much time that
could be spent out of doors.

As for my work, teaching is a fine and two-way thing. But
done too much without refreshment, it can also keep one sta-
tionary and static, locked into present knowledge and its repeti-
tion: fine for some, but it pales for me. Literary distinction, too, is
illusory—if someone reads what I write now and then, is affected
by it, and responds, I am deeply gratified. That's the best part of
the practice, and the most I can reasonably hope for. Of course
I will keep on writing. But it is no profession to depend on in
material terms, nor is it an adequate end in itself, at least for me.
I love my family, my friends, my dwelling place, and my library,
and I hope and intend to devote a goodly portion of my time
and attention to all of them, as long as I remain able. What else
does that leave?

What I would really like to do is to devote most of my days—
as fits nicely with the many outdoor chores an old place like this
requires—to the deep study of this tiny slice of the world. The
fly fauna here is phenomenal: I've always wanted to become a
dipterist. And the other insects—I don't even know our bumble-
bees, for cripe's sake! Or most of our moths, or mosses, nor even
all the mollusks. This is simply sinful, after thirty years here. As
one who is called a naturalist, what I most want now, is to really
become a naturalist.

A young writer friend, to whom I recently explained my

ambition to become a deeper naturalist, asked me, "To what end?" That made me think. I suppose at a time when activism has never been more needed, the pursuit of pure natural history (like pure art) might strike some as self-indulgent, even merely masturbatory: harmless enough, but unhelpful to the revolution, useless to the resistance against our clear and present crisis. Or is it? Just as pure (or basic) science has come up with essential solutions at least as often as applied science, so has unpremeditated natural history revealed what we've needed to know again and again. Who knows when a given encounter, closely observed, might uncover some generality that applies to specific questions or problems all over? For example, the long search for the cryptic nest of the marbled murrelet finally led to mossy boughs in remnant old-growth forests near the northwestern coast. Along with its famous fellow old-growth obligate, the northern spotted owl, and its lesser-known cohort, the Hemphill's jumping slug, the murrelet now drives much of Pacific Northwest timber management policy through its natural history. At the very least, if communicated, each naturalist's findings add to the simmering pot of knowledge that might someday allow us to behave in an adaptive manner after all.

But must any such practical justification really be invoked? Isn't it enough that the pursuit of deep natural history is one of the surest paths toward an entirely earthly state of enlightenment? In a 1969 interview with Robert Tabozzi, Vladimir Nabokov said, "The emotion of recognizing in an alpine meadow a butterfly one knows to be different from another and whose special comportment one observes—this emotion is a feeling in which the scientific and the artistic sides join in an apex of sharp pleasure unknown to the man walking under trees he cannot even name."

Surely the inability of even educated people to name the

trees beneath which they walk presents a distinct and timely danger to our culture and its future, if any. Where, in a populace innocent of sincere acquaintance with its extra-human neighbors, is the ability to live well in our shared neighborhood to come from? And where will conservationists come from, when the young no longer meet the world in special places of dirt and leaf and water and crawler? I believe with burning urgency that our ecological illiteracy is not only lazy, self-impugning, and solipsistic to the max, but also ultimately suicidal.

Yet the ignorance of the population at large is not what this essay is really about. It is about how I, or anyone, might aspire toward lesser ignorance. After all, it is important to remember that depth is a relative thing. For one person to learn his neighborhood birds might be the objective; for another, the butterflies in her garden. No one need feel compelled to attempt the impossible. The point is to get to know a few new lives, then take it as deep as you want. Intimidated by the bounty of life that they can never hope to know in its entirety, most folks give up before they ever make a start. Others pick up a field guide, and begin.

The final three essays respond to the H. J. Andrews Experimental Forest, a dense coniferous forest often cloaked in patient rain, tucked in the western foothills of Oregon's Cascades. The Andrews is the research site that gave birth to the modern ecological study of old-growth forests. It was later designated an LTER site—part of a federal network for Long Term Ecological Research. At sites representative of many major habitats in North America and beyond, the National Science Foundation has committed to examine ecological change over the course of many human generations. More recently, transdisciplinary collaborators Kathleen Dean Moore, a philosopher; Fred Swanson, a geomorphologist and ecologist; and Charles Goodrich, a poet, developed a corollary project to extend the LTER's reach. (Both Moore and Goodrich are contributors to this book.) Believing it was as important to honor and record human emotional response to this place as it was to study ecological change, they initiated the Long Term Ecological Reflections program. Cosponsored by the Spring Creek Project for Ideas, Nature, and the Written Word at Oregon State University and the U.S. Forest Service, the reflections project is designed to last two hundred years, bringing writers into the Andrews to pay attention to the interplay of psyche and forest. The two LTER projects interweave, recording the ecological dynamics of this forest and people's relationship with it.

Attending to the Beautiful
Mess of the World

When the fifth and sixth graders from the McKenzie River Christian School arrive at forest headquarters, each kid wears a name tag made from a slice of wood that looks like a sugar cookie. The cookies hang around their necks, announcing the camp names they have chosen for the field trip: Fang, Dark Dragon, Caos, Monkey Girl, Money Maker. They show little interest in the weather station that measures temperature, wind, chemistry of rain, weight of snow, the sensors downloading data every hour. They perk up at the sight of a stainless steel mercury collector, the tank sporting robotic arms that slide its cover into place to protect a rain sample. They don't seem to hear the weatherman's words as I copy them down in my field notebook. "Rain in Ohio comes down strong as vinegar and eats paint." "Some of the best rain in America comes down right here in Oregon." The kids shuffle, uninterested in the meteorologist's homily.

Asked if they ever have seen an old-growth forest, the children look blankly at their guide. These children live in the shade of five-hundred-year-old Douglas-firs. How can it be that they do not recognize these giant beings that live in their neighborhood, that have stood here, tough and serene, since before science discovered its method?

Freed from the entrapment of an adult lecture, the kids tumble like puppies down the forest lane. When one spots the rough-skinned newt sauntering on wet asphalt, they all freeze, stare, and go silent, magnetized by the oddness of its orange belly, brown back, and translucent handlike appendages. They especially love hearing that the newt is poisonous, that after handling it they must all wash their hands. They love the danger, the taming power of the small. It sets loose a featherweight bout of animal stories.

"That's nothing. You should see the Pacific giants!" says Fang, gesturing wider than his torso to demonstrate their impressive size. He recounts how the salamanders, black and vicious, swaggered up when he and his father went fishing, how they grabbed the fish guts, thrashing their heads all around like monsters to consume the slime.

"Yeah? Well, I've seen lamprey eels that swam up the McKenzie all the way into Lookout Creek!" brags Caos. He points to the rivulet tumbling past the parking lot.

The newt has brought them back from their boredom into what Walt Whitman called the "costless, divine, original concrete."

I have come to spend a week at the H. J. Andrews Experimental Forest, one of twenty-six Long Term Ecological Research sites ranging from Alaska to the Caribbean to Antarctica funded by the National Science Foundation. The Andrews, flanking the western slope of the Cascade Range, occupies the drainage basin of Lookout Creek, a tributary of the Blue River, the McKenzie River, the Willamette, and finally the Columbia, which dumps out into the Pacific Ocean. This is one of the most studied forests in the world, a 15,000-acre research site established in 1948, when "sawlog foresters" helped the postwar nation rebuild through a grand investment on the domestic front.

Among the forest's more famous subjects of scrutiny are dead logs. Begun in 1985, the log decomposition study focuses on two-foot-diameter timbers placed on the forest floor to rot. The project will last two hundred years, the time projected for natural processes to turn the tree trunks to dirt. Every month or so researchers slice a giant cookie off the end of the logs. They take note of rot, fungus, bark beetles. They analyze the cookies in the lab. Dead logs are one of the most critical components of the forest ecosystem within the first few years of the tree's death, as organisms take advantage of new resources. Ongoing studies will look at how much nutrition logs contribute to the forest and how much carbon dioxide they release into the atmosphere. The study spawned the term "morticulture," connoting that attention to the dead has relevance to the nurture of the living.

Another celebrity of the Andrews is the northern spotted owl, a keystone species for Pacific Northwest forest health. If owls go, that loss is a sign that an essential life supporting complexity has gone. The northern spotted owl has been vilified, polemicized, eco-terrorized, and reduced to the size of a bumper sticker. Eco-extremists who advocate a no-touch purity for the forest haven't helped by sabotaging forest road lockboxes with broken glass and, in one case, a loaded firearm aimed at the ranger unlocking the box. Pragmatists say that more loggers have lost their jobs to the industrialization of logging and plywood manufacture than to ecosystem protection. Try asking a lumberjack on unemployment to take comfort in that reasoning. It's easier for him to blame the regulator than the operator who might give him a job. The phrase "northern spotted owl" barely refers to the creature any longer, so debased has it become with political rhetoric. Who still sees the owl when its name is spoken? I'm drawn to the place in order to detox from such politics, to see the bird, and try to bear witness to the terms of its existence.

I welcomed the invitation to spend time in the experimental forest and participate in a new project, Long Term Ecological Reflections, spurred by philosopher Kathleen Dean Moore and geologist Fred Swanson, a concomitant to scientific work being done under the umbrella of Long Term Ecological Research. I am participating in a two-hundred-year-long experiment bringing writers and poets into the forest to sample key research sites and spend time with scientists in the field. My only obligation is to observe, reflect, and write. In science an experiment is governed by a method. There are controls, limitations, rules, hypotheses. It must produce empirical evidence. Its conclusions must be verifiable, repeatable by another scientist. An experiment in science adds to collective knowledge. Earth is round, not flat, and circles the sun. Nearly everyone on Earth knows this, one would hope, and these facts are not subject to reasonable argument, aesthetic judgment, or cultural relativism.

In correspondence I asked Fred Swanson what he means when he uses the word "experiment."

"Funny you should ask," he replied. "Some local scientists have been discussing this (with some heat). In a narrow science sense an experiment uses alternative treatments to test hypotheses—properties of a standard agronomic experiment include several rather different treatments (for example, levels of fertilization or cutting), replication (multiple plots with the same treatment), random assignment of treatments to plots, pre-treatment measurements . . .

"On the other hand," Swanson continued, "we have the more casual use of experiment, as if just trying something out and seeing how it works. In field ecology and geology it can be very difficult to conduct good experiments. One usually just starts out observing to get the drift of how the world is working. Creative flashes in science often step beyond the rigidity of the experimental process, coming in leaps of wonderment and faith."

In poetry an experiment is governed by freedom. It dispenses with received forms, levels of diction, metrical conventions, and even syntactical rules. It may favor process over product, music over meaning, disjunction over coherence. It is unique, unrepeatable. An experiment in poetry adds to the sense of depth, complexity, mystery, and feeling in the world. If there is a "poetic method," it is to free oneself from method and enter into the excitement of creating something new and true to a very individual experience and voice. Poetry's more subversive practitioners (from Dada to homophonic translation to Flarf) challenge rationality through pranks, games, and erasure of artistic "value." They use method to leap beyond method, perhaps in the same way scientists often make their surprise findings through leaps.

The hope in the Andrews is that by careful and sustained observation, a testimony on behalf of the forest will help to keep it alive—and that applied science and applied humanities will braid a solid working relationship. But I wondered, if poetry is to be the equal partner of science in this project, would I need a hypothesis?

On a warm May afternoon, Fred drives me upslope along Forest Road 130 behind the Andrews headquarters through a collage of forest types that are the result of varied logging strategies tried out over recent years. He is a tall, lean timber of a man, gray-bearded as the licheny Northwest trees, with a gentle yet intense manner. He tells me about the sites he'd like me to visit. "You might want to go sit on that gravel bar in Lookout Creek." It feels more like conversation than instruction, though I know each writer who comes over the duration of the project will be asked to visit the same locations: creek, log decomp, and clear-cut sites. I'm expecting science to be the boss here. After all, my host has been studying this terrain for decades. It takes me a few interchanges before I realize that he really means to make me a partner in the enterprise of understanding this place.

We park at the Blue River Face timber sale unit, an area partially cut one year, then burned the next, and planted with seedlings the following year. The cutting prescription was set on a 180-year rotation with 30 percent live tree retention. Fewer cuts were made close to the river to decrease erosion and silting. Snags were left standing as habitat for voles and flying squirrels.

Fred strides down into the cut, peering at stumps, scanning the tree rings for signs of an earlier wildfire in these firs that had lived five hundred years. I wander along the charred ground, trying to hold onto his language for the place. I write "patch cutting," "too much edge," "min frag," "owl injunction," "new forestry." Fred has an excited mind and verbal acuity that are hard to keep up with, especially when his commentary is filled with a lifetime of learning about this forest. What really interests him are volcanoes. He calls himself a "closet volcanologist." He's visited eruptions in Hawai'i, the Galápagos Islands, and Mount St. Helens to see how such a scale of disturbance registers in the forest. He says that "the organism perceives the mechanism of disturbance and makes a genetic interpretation of the mechanism."

Ten days after Mount St. Helens blew off her top, leveling everything within an eight-mile radius, the entire terrain white with ash from the fire and pyroclastic flows, he watched colleagues digging holes to study the deposits. He happened to gaze down into one. He saw spidery, translucent threads of mycorrhizal fungi fluttering in the wind, threads so fine he couldn't have seen them if they had not been dusted with fine volcanic ash. Ten days after the cataclysm, the forest had raced back to work. It was as if fire had said to the Earth, "Go forth and multiply."

Fred rejoins me at the roadside where I've been standing to study the landscape, a gentle slope leading toward the seam below where water must be flowing and tiers of brocaded hillsides rising beyond.

"What do you see?" he asks. There's a beat or two of silence in which I realize that my lack of experience and specialized language are part of his hypothesis in this collaborative experiment.

"It looks messy. There's brush left on the ground, tree-sized logs, snags. It looks natural," I answer. "This landscape reminds me of our family's summer home in Canada where we haven't cut anything for fifty years. Unless it threatened to fall on our house. The woods there is such a mess of overgrowth and downfall, you can hardly make your way through it anymore. I've come to think of nature unhindered as messy."

I try to describe what I notice at the cut site. Brush, snag, stump, char, feathery seedlings, bear grass, salal, tiny red-stalked clusters of something that grows dense as streptococcus on an agar plate.

"Yes," he says, "the whole landscape is organizing itself."

A flash of words pops into my mind, giving shape to something I've felt for years.

"This cut keeps intact the wisdom of Earth. Nature, to me, means deep time—what the Earth has learned through long trial and error."

"Of course, I'm speaking poetically," I add apologetically, imagining how useless such words would be in a grant application to the National Science Foundation. Yet as a poet working in the house of science, I feel responsible to bear forward some remnant of the romantic tradition, the sense that out of the particular the transcendent may arise and that language can embody such experience. The poet of our time has a more complicated task. She lives with a divided mind, remaining as skeptical as a scientist about the tools of her trade. Hasn't language been used to manipulate, oppress, deceive, and betray our ideals more consistently than it has ever served as a vessel for poetic or spiritual feeling? How can poetic language be called to the world's aid during these days of threat and peril? Can poetry carry our love as a mine canary into the world? This last question must be my hypothesis in this collaborative experiment.

Fred nods and explains the site this way.

"In the current ecological approach to forestry you try to keep more of the complexity of nature in the disturbance you create. A little bit of chaos is a good thing."

We talk about the failures of language in both purviews, how so little of what we've said and done has protected what we love. When the Northwest Forest Plan was written, its architects looked for words to describe the forests they hoped to save from the blade so that the land could fulfill its fullest evolutionary possibility.

Ancient forest. Virgin forest. Old growth. Everyone agreed that if those words were the best they could do to inspire conservation, the last stands of North America's forest legacy were doomed.

"Is this a good landscape or a bad landscape?" Fred asks as we gaze over the green tapestry. I'm speechless. I want to think that beauty makes a landscape good, but that trivializes the complexity that makes life work. This mess too is good for the precious attention it brings out in us.

I thread my gaze through the scrub, slash, and snags. So much of the process of regeneration on disturbed land occurs beyond the apprehension of the senses. There is a wholeness to a forest that the damaged forest cannot help but seek. Such a process is a fruitful laboratory for the daydreams of scientist and poet alike, as we reach for the words to describe what lies just past our comprehension. What is going on out there might be described by a graph, an equation, a poem sequence, or a conversation. All would fall short of explaining the complexity of relationships that comprise a forest. That gap between the desire to know the world intimately and our capacity to do so is one the attentive mind is always drawn to fill. Paying attention here means more than engaging in focused study. It means "attending to," as one would do in the care of one's home, livestock, or beloved.

The next morning Steve Akers and I clamber over vine maple and Oregon grape, a tangled mess of scrub that covers Hardy Ridge high over Cougar Reservoir. This terrain is better suited to flying squirrels and red-backed voles than to a mildly arthritic, bipedal primate. But here I am on a sun-drenched morning in May, hiking with the head of the northern spotted owl research team and filled with unaccountable joy. Last night Steve had been bushwhacking toward an owl that was calling from a mile away. He set a compass point and hiked into the dark forest toward the call but never found the bird. He's been working on the owl study for seven years, on wildlife fieldwork for twenty-one. Today we're looking for a spotted owl that has been in the study for twelve years, one habituated to the visits of field scientists.

Extensive study of this species had been conducted for at least a decade prior to its 1990 designation as threatened under the Endangered Species Act. The northern spotted owl is one of the most studied birds in the world, inspiring unprecedented collaboration among scientists, governmental agencies, universities, and private landowners.

We break into the opening shade by a small stand of firs—trees not as super old, as we've seen along the McKenzie River Trail, where there are giants over six hundred years old, but stately elders nonetheless. The ground is dappled with light, the air cool and damp. The hillside drops steeply away below us. Ahead of me Steve hoots the four-note location call: *Hooh-hoohoo-hooh.* The last syllable descends with a slight warble. No response. Then he turns, and a quiet smile opens on his face. He has the bright and easy look of a man who knows how lucky he is to love his work. He points over my left shoulder.

Silent, she's perched on a small understory branch twenty feet up. She's watching us, waiting for us to notice her. She knows the contract. She will give us data: we will give her mice. After three decades of research on the spotted owl, scientists have gained a wealth of understanding about this creature's life history. Each spring the field crew checks nesting pairs for their reproductive status and bands fledglings to include them in future surveys. The data gathered led in 1994 to the Northwest Forest Plan, a comprehensive guide to conservation that decreased the rate of logging and how the cutting is done, giving the owls and their entire ecosystem a better chance at survival.

But data cannot compare to the experience of that deep well of attention, quiet, and presence that is the owl. She has a spotted breast, long barred tail, and tawny facial disks with brown semicircles fringing her face and back-to-back white parentheses framing her eyes. These markings give the impression that her eyes are the size of her head. The blackness of her pupils is so pure they look like portals into the universe.

When Steve takes the first mouse out of his aerated Tupperware container, lifting it by its tail and placing it on a log, the owl drops, silent as air, down through the branches and closes her talons. She lofts back up to the branch and scans around. She may be looking to see if a goshawk is near. Whatever constitutes a threat to her does not include us. How rare it is to have more than a fleeting glimpse of a creature in the wild. Still clutching the mouse, she burps up a pellet that plops to the ground, gives us a nonchalant look, then gulps down her meal.

"You want to see the parachute-drop?" Steve asks with a grin. The white mice have been raised in captivity, and their sense of space has been so constrained that when he unsnaps the lid, they stretch their heads up and look around but make no attempt to run away. The world to them is the size of the container in which they find themselves. He places the second mouse onto the log, and the owl billows out her wings, buoying herself down to us. It takes a moment to understand why her flight catches me each time by surprise. No riffle, no flutter of resistance through the feathers. She's evolved for this easy drop onto her prey. The spotted owl is a sit-and-wait hunter, unlike the goshawk, which will tear through the woods in pursuit. The fringed edge of her wing reduces noise and increases drag, making this strategy a good match of form with function.

Steve collects the pellet, and we poke the slimy gray glob of indigestible fur and bones from the previous day's meal. The bones are very delicate, still shiny with the life that left them, some nearly two inches long.

"Maybe a wood rat," Steve says. Through binoculars he can see the owl's identification band. Last year a male was keeping this female company, a two-year-old from nearby King Creek. This year, so far, she appears to be alone. The owl team's last visit to this site was one month ago.

"How about the side grab?" He might be a dad boasting about the agility of his soccer-playing daughter. He isn't making the owl perform for our enjoyment. These flight skills are as natural to the owl as stepping over a crack in a sidewalk is for us. The next mouse is barely out of his hand, scurrying in confusion on the tree trunk that rises beside me, when the owl swoops down, talons leading, and picks it off right beside my shoulder. The catch happens so fast that she's flying away by the time I realize she's grabbed the prey, killing it instantly in her grip. She flies up to a snag broken off forty feet above the ground and tucks the mouse carefully into the jagged wood. This is a cache, not a nest. If she'd been delivering food to her young, the nest would be a natural platform high in a tree. She checks to be sure the mouse is well hidden. If she does have nestlings, she'll come back later for takeout.

The spotted owl research protocol demands that we spend an hour with the bird. She's had her limit of commercially raised albino mice, so now we sit to see what she does and if what she does will tell us whether she has a mate or nestlings. This suits my research protocol just fine. I like to watch. The owl doesn't make a sound. She perches on a branch maybe twenty feet above us. She is still. She watches us. She reaches her head forward—"the pre-pounce lean," Steve calls the gesture—as if she has seen some prey on the ground. The song of a thrush flutters through the quiet, the auditory equivalent of seeing an orchid in the forest. Beauty is what I came here for, a beauty enhanced, not diminished, by science. If I had only my senses to work with, how much thinner would the experience be? What a record we might have of the world's hidden beauty if field scientists and poets routinely spent time in one another's company.

A young tree, broken and caught between two others, creaks to the rhythm of the wind. How well the owl must know this sound. Does she anticipate the crash of its falling? What is the consciousness of a spotted owl? There she perches perceiving us, and here we sit perceiving her. We exchange the long, slow interspecies stare—no fear, no threat, only the confusing mystery of the Other. Steve knows her language well enough to speak a few words: the location call, the bark of aggression. Perhaps that means she thinks we are owls. We do not look like owls. But we do, briefly, behave like owls, catching and offering prey, being still, and turning our eyes to the forest.

"What are you?"

"What are *you*?"

That's the conversation we have with our eyes.

"What will you do next?"

"What will *you* do next?"

I keep falling into the owl's eyes.

Then we stand up and hike down from that high place.

An idea common to science and poetry is that an experiment is an act the outcome of which is unknown. In science the goal is to add to a body of knowledge. In poetry the goal is to add to a body of reflection, to share the innerness of human life in ways that helps us to get the drift of how the world is working. Who can know what the outcome will be of such practices when poet and scientist attempt to engage in them side by side, not one in service to the other, but both in service to the promise of discovery and connection?

Witness to the Rain

This Oregon rain at the start of winter falls steadily in sheets of gray. Falling unimpeded, it makes a gentle hiss. You'd think that rain falls equally over the land, but it doesn't. The rhythm and the tempo change markedly from place to place. As I stand in a tangle of salal and Oregon grape, the rain strikes a *ratatatat* on the hard, shiny leaves, the snare drum of sclerophylls. Rhododendron leaves, broad and flat, receive the rain with a smack that makes the leaf bounce and rebound, dancing in the downpour. Beneath this massive hemlock, the drops are fewer, and the craggy trunk knows rain as dribbles down its furrows. On bare soil the rain splats on the clay, while fir needles swallow it up with an audible gulp.

In contrast, the fall of rain on moss is nearly silent. I kneel among them, sinking into their softness to watch and to listen. The drops are so quick that my eye is always chasing, but not catching, their arrival. At last, by narrowing my gaze to just a single frond and staring, I see it. The impact bows the shoot downward, but the drop itself vanishes. It is soundless. There is no drip or splash, but I can see the front of water move, darkening the stem as it is drunk in and silently dissipated among the tiny shingled leaves.

Most other places I know, water is a discrete entity. It is hemmed in by well-defined boundaries: lakeshores, stream banks, or the great rocky coastline. You can stand at its edge and say "This is water" and "This is land." Those fish and those tadpoles are of the water realm; these trees, these mosses, and these four-leggeds are creatures of the land. But here in these misty forests those edges seem to blur: rain so fine and constant as to be indistinguishable from air, cedars wrapped with cloud so dense that only their outline forms emerge. Water doesn't seem to make a clear distinction between gaseous phase and liquid. The air merely touches a leaf or a tendril of my hair, and suddenly a drop appears.

Even the river, Lookout Creek, doesn't respect clear boundaries. The surface flow tumbles and slides down the main channel, where a cocky black dipper rides the current between pools. Fred Swanson, a hydrologist here at the Andrews Experimental Forest, has told me of another stream, the invisible shadow of Lookout Creek. This water, the "hyporheic flow," moves under the stream, through cobble beds and old sandbars. It edges up the toe slope to the forest, a wide unseen river that flows beneath the eddies and the splash, a deep invisible river, known only to roots and rocks, intimate beyond our knowing. It is hyporheic flow that I'm listening for.

Wandering along the banks of Lookout Creek, I lean up against an old cedar with my back nestled in its curves and try to imagine the currents below. But all I sense is water dripping down my neck. Every branch is weighted down with mossy curtains of *Isothecium*, and droplets hang from the tangled ends, just as they hang from my hair. When I bend my head over, I can see them both. But the droplets on *Isothecium* are far bigger than the drops on my bangs. In fact, the drops of moss water seem larger than any I know, and they hang, swelling and pregnant with gravity, far longer than the drops on me, or on twigs or bark. They dangle and rotate, reflecting the entire forest and a woman in a bright yellow slicker.

I'm not sure I can trust what I'm seeing. I wish I had a set of calipers, so that I could measure the drops of moss water and see if they really are bigger. I take refuge in the play of the scientist part of myself, spinning out hypotheses. Perhaps the high humidity around moss makes the drops last longer? Maybe in residence among mosses, raindrops absorb some property that increases their surface tension, making it stronger against the pull of gravity? Perhaps it's just an illusion, like how the full moon looks so much bigger at the horizon. Does the diminutive scale of the moss leaves make the drops appear larger? After hours in the penetrating rain, I am suddenly damp and chilled. The path back to the cabin is a temptation. I could so easily retreat to tea and dry clothes, but I cannot pull myself away. However alluring the thought of warmth, there is no substitute for standing in the rain to waken every sense—senses that are muted within four walls, where my attention would be on *me*, instead of all that is more than me. Inside looking out, I could not bear the loneliness of being dry in a wet world. Here in the rainforest, I don't want to just be a witness to rain, passive and protected. I want to be part of the downpour, to be soaked, along with the dark humus that squishes underfoot. I wish that I could stand like a shaggy cedar with rain seeping into my bark, that water could dissolve the barrier between us. I want to feel what they feel and know what they know.

But I am not a cedar, and I am cold. Surely there are places where the warm-blooded among us take refuge. I poke my head into an undercut bank by the stream, but its back wall runs with rivulets. No shelter there, nor in the hollow of a tree-fall where I hoped the upturned roots would slow the rain. A spiderweb hangs between two dangling roots. Even this is filled, a silken hammock cradling a spoonful of water. My hopes rise where the vine maples are bent low to form a moss-draped dome. I push aside the gauzy curtain and stoop to enter the tiny dark room, roofed with layers of moss. It's quiet and windless, just big enough for one. The light comes through the moss-woven roof like pinprick stars, but so do the drips.

As I walk back to the trail, a giant log blocks the way. It has fallen from the toe slope out into the river, where its branches drag in the rising current. Its top rests on the opposite shore. Going under looks easier than going over, so I drop to my hands and knees. And here I find my dry place. The ground mosses are brown and dry, the soil soft and powdery. The log makes a roof overhead more than a meter wide in the wedge-shaped space where the slope falls away to the stream. I can stretch out my legs, the slope angle perfectly accommodating the length of my back. I let my head rest in a dry nest of *Hylocomium* moss and sigh in contentment. My breath forms a cloud above me, up where brown tufts of moss still cling to the furrowed bark, embroidered with spiderwebs and wisps of lichen that haven't seen the sun since this tree became a log. This log inches above my face weighs many tons. All that keeps it from seeking its natural angle of repose upon my chest is a hinge of fractured wood at the stump and cracked branches propped on the other side of the stream. Those supports could give way at any moment. And one day they will. But given the fast tempo of raindrops and the slow tempo of tree-falls, I feel safe in the moment. The pace of my resting and the pace of its falling run on different clocks.

Time as objective reality has never made much sense to me. It's only what happens that matters. How can minutes and years, devices of our own creation, mean the same thing to gnats and to cedars? Two hundred years is young for the trees, whose tops this morning are hung with mist. It's an eyeblink of time for the river and nothing at all for the rocks. The rocks and the river and these very same trees will likely be here in another two hundred years, if we take good care. As for me and that chipmunk and the cloud of gnats milling in a shaft of sunlight, we will have moved on.

If there is meaning in the past and in the imagined future, it is captured in the moment. When you have all the time in the world, you can spend it, not on going somewhere, but on being where you are. So I stretch out, close my eyes, and listen to the rain.

The cushiony moss keeps me warm and dry, and I roll over on my elbow to look out on the wet world. The drops fall heavily on a patch of *Mnium insigne*, right at eye level. This moss stands upright, nearly two inches tall. The leaves are broad and rounded, like a fig tree in miniature. One leaf among the many draws my eye by its long tapered tip, so unlike the rounded edges of the others. As I lean in closer, my head lines up with the drip line of the log, and drips trickle down my neck, but no matter. The threadlike tip of the leaf is moving, animated in a most un-plantlike fashion. The thread seems firmly anchored to the apex of the moss leaf, an extension of its pellucid green. But the tip is circling, waving in the air as if it is searching for something. Its motion reminds me of the way inchworms will rise up on their hind sucker feet and wave their long bodies about until they encounter the adjacent twig, to which they then attach their forelegs, release their back legs, and arch across the gulf of empty space. But this is no many-legged caterpillar; it is a shiny green filament, a moss thread animal, lit from within like a fiber-optic element. As I watch, the wandering thread touches upon a leaf just millimeters away. It seems to tap several times at the new leaf, and then, as if reassured, it stretches itself out across the gap. It holds like a taut green cable, more than doubling its initial length. For just a moment, the two mosses are bridged by the shining green thread; then green light flows like a river across the bridge and vanishes, lost in the greenness of the moss. Is that not grace, to see an animal made of green light and water, a mere thread of a being who, like me, has gone walking in the rain?

Down by the river, I stand and listen. The sound of individual raindrops is lost in the foaming white rush and smooth glide over rock. If you didn't know better, you might not recognize raindrops and rivers as kin, so different are the particular and the collective. I lean over a still pool, reach my hand in, and let the drops fall from my fingers, just to be sure.

Alder leaves lie fallen on the gravel, their drying edges upturned to form leafy cups. Rainwater has pooled in several leaves and is stained red-brown, like tea, with tannins leached from the leaf. Strands of lichen lie scattered among them where the wind has torn them free. Suddenly I see the experiment I need to test my hypothesis; the materials are neatly laid out before me. I find two strands of lichen, equal in size and length, and blot them on my flannel shirt inside my raincoat. One strand I place in the leaf cup of red alder tea; the other I soak in a pool of pure rainwater. Slowly I lift them both up, side by side, and watch the droplets form at the ends of the moss strands. Sure enough, they are different. The plain water forms small, rapid drops that seem in a hurry to let go. But the droplets steeped in alder water grow large, heavy, and hang for a long moment before gravity pulls them away. I feel the grin spreading over my face with the "Aha!" moment. There *are* different kinds of drops, depending on the relationship between the water and the plant. If tannin-rich alder water increases the size of the drops, might not water seeping through a long curtain of moss also pick up tannins, making the big strong drops I thought I was seeing? One thing I've learned in the woods is that there is no such thing as random. Everything is steeped in meaning, colored by relationships, one with another.

Where new gravel meets old shore, a still pool has formed beneath the overhanging trees. Cut off from the main channel, it fills from the rise of hyporheic flow, the water rising from below to fill the shallow basin, where summer daisies look surprised to be submerged two feet deep now that the rains have come. In summer, this pool was a flowery swale; now it is a sunken meadow that tells of the river's transition from low braided channel to the full banks of winter. It is a different river in August than in October. You'd have to stand here a long time to know them both, and even longer to know the river that was here before the coming of the gravel bar, and the river that will be after it leaves.

Perhaps we cannot know the river. But what about the drops? I stand for a long time, by the still backwater pool and listen. It is a mirror for the falling rain and is textured all over by its fine and steady fall. I strain to hear only rain whisper among the many sounds, and find that I can. It arrives with a high sprickley sound, a *shurring* so light that it only blurs the glassy surface but does not disrupt the reflection. The pool is overhung with branches of vine maple reaching from the shore, a low spray of hemlock, and from the gravel bar, alder stems incline over the edge. Water falls from each of these trees into the pool, each to its own rhythm. The hemlock makes a rapid pulse. Water collects on every needle, but travels to the branch tips before falling, running to the drip line, where it releases in a steady *pit, pit, pit, pit, pit,* drawing a dotted line in the water below.

Maple stems shed their water much differently. The drips from maple are big and heavy. I watch them form and then plummet to the surface of the pool. They hit with such force that the drop makes a deep and hollow sound. *Bloink.* The rebound causes the water to jump from the surface, so it looks as if it were erupting from below. There are sporadic bloinks beneath the maples. Why is this drop so different from the hemlock drips? I step in close to watch the way that water moves on maple. The drops don't form just anywhere along the stem. They arise mostly where past years' bud scars have formed a tiny ridge. The rainwater sheets over the smooth green bark and gets dammed up behind the wall of the bud scar. It swells and gathers until it tops the little dam and spills over, tumbling in a massive drop to the water below. *Bloink.*

Sshhhh from rain, *pitpitpit* from hemlock, *bloink* from maple, and finally *popp* of falling alder water. Alder drops make a slow music. It takes time for fine rain to traverse the scabrous rough surface of an alder leaf. It's not as big as a maple drop, not big enough to splash, but its *popp* ripples the surface and sends out concentric rings. I close my eyes and listen to the voices of the rain.

The reflecting surface of the pool is textured with their signatures, each one different in pace and resonance. Every drip, it seems, is changed by its relationship with life, whether it encounters moss or maple or fir bark or my hair. And we think of it as simply rain, as if it were one thing, as if we understood it. I think that moss knows rain better than we do, and so do maples. Maybe there is no such thing as rain; there are only raindrops, each with its own story.

Listening to rain, time disappears. If time is measured by the period between events, alder drip time is different from maple drop. This forest is textured with different kinds of time, as the surface of the pool is dimpled with different kinds of rain. Fir needles fall with the high-frequency hiss of rain, branches fall with the *bloink* of big drops, and trees with a rare but thunderous thud. Rare, unless you measure time like a river. And we think of it as simply time, as if it were one thing, as if we understood it. Maybe there is no such thing as time; there are only moments, each with its own story.

I can see my face reflected in a dangling drop. The fish-eye lens gives me a giant forehead and tiny ears. I suppose that's the way we are as humans, thinking too much and listening too little. By paying attention we acknowledge that we have something to learn from intelligences not our own. By listening, standing witness, we create an openness to the world in which the boundaries between us can dissolve in a raindrop. The drop swells on the tip of a cedar, and I catch it on my tongue like a blessing.

Mind in the Forest

I touch trees as others might stroke the fenders of automobiles or finger silk fabrics or fondle cats. Trees do not purr, do not flatter, do not inspire a craving for ownership or power. They stand their ground, immune to merely human urges. Saplings yield under the weight of a hand and then spring back when the hand lifts away, but mature trees accept one's touch without so much as a shiver. While I am drawn to all ages and kinds, from maple sprouts barely tall enough to hold their leaves off the ground to towering sequoias with their crowns wreathed in fog, I am especially drawn to the ancient, battered ones, the survivors.

Recently I spent a week in the company of ancient trees. The season was October and the site was the H. J. Andrews Experimental Forest, a 15,800-acre research area defined by the drainage basin of Lookout Creek, within Willamette National Forest, on the western slope of the Cascade Mountains in Oregon. It's a wet place. At higher elevations in the Andrews, annual precipitation averages 140 inches, and even the lower elevations receive 90 inches, twice the amount that falls on my well-watered home region of southern Indiana. Unlike Indiana's hardwood hills, this is conifer country. The oldest of the Douglas-firs, western hemlocks, western red cedars, and Pacific yews that flourish here range in age from five hundred to eight hundred years, veterans of countless fires, windstorms, landslides, insect infestations, and floods.

On the first morning of my stay, I follow a trail through moist bottomland from my lodging in the headquarters compound toward Lookout Creek, where I plan to spend half an hour or so in meditation. The morning fog is thick, so the treetops merge with gray sky. Condensation drips from every needle and leaf. My breath steams. Lime-green lichens, some as long as a horse's tail, dangle from branches. Set off against the somber greens and browns of the conifers, the yellow and red leaves of vine maples, bigleaf maples, and dogwoods appear luminous despite the damp. Shelf fungi jut from the sides of old stumps like tiny balconies, and hemlock sprigs glisten from nurse logs. The undergrowth is as dense as a winter pelt.

Along the way, I reach out to brush my fingers over dozens of big trees, but I keep moving, intent on my destination. Then I come upon a Douglas-fir whose massive trunk, perhaps four feet in diameter at chest height, is surrounded by scaffolding, which provides a stage for rope-climbing by scientists and visiting schoolchildren. Something about this tree—its patience, its generosity, its dignity—stops me. I place my palms and forehead against the furrowed, moss-covered bark, and rest there for a spell. Gradually the agitation of travel seeps out of me and calm seeps in. Only after I stand back and open my eyes, and notice how the fog has begun to burn off, do I realize that my contact with this great tree must have lasted fifteen or twenty minutes.

I continue on to a gravel bar on Lookout Creek, a jumble of boulders, cobbles, pebbles, and grit scoured loose from the volcanic plateau that forms the base of the Cascade Mountains. Because these mountains are young, the slopes are steep and the water moves fast. Even the largest boulders have been tumbled and rounded. Choosing one close to a riffle, I sit cross-legged and half-close my eyes, and I am enveloped in water sounds, a ruckus from upstream and a burbling from downstream. Now and again I hear the thump of a rock shifting in the flow, a reminder that the whole mountain range is sliding downhill, chunk by chunk, grain by grain.

Although I have tried meditating for shorter or longer stretches since my college days, forty years ago, I have never been systematic about the practice, nor have I ever been good at quieting what Buddhists call the monkey mind. Here beside Lookout Creek, however, far from my desk and duties, with no task ahead of me but that of opening myself to this place, I settle quickly. I begin by following my breath, the oldest rhythm of flesh, but soon I am following the murmur of the creek, and I am gazing at the bright leaves of maples and dogwoods that glow along the thread of the stream like jewels on a necklace, and I am watching light gleam on water shapes formed by current slithering over rocks, and for a spell I disappear; there is only this rapt awareness.

When the H. J. Andrews Experimental Forest was established in 1948, what we now call "old growth" was labeled on maps as "large saw-timber." The original purpose of the forest was to determine the best methods of harvesting big trees. The assumption was that they should be cut down—the only question was how. Fortunately, since 1948, many people, both inside and outside the U.S. Forest Service, have come to see that venerable trees possess values other than supplying lumber.

Research conducted at the Andrews has taught us much of

what we know about old growth in the Pacific Northwest. In addition to stands of ancient trees, the watershed contains naturally burned areas, open glades, recovering clear-cuts, and managed research plots. Some of these plots are devoted to studying the effects of various harvesting practices. But of the more than one hundred experiments currently under way, many focus on the role of forests in protecting water quality, controlling stream flow and sedimentation, cycling and storing carbon, and providing habitat for wildlife, including endangered species such as the northern spotted owl.

Aside from these ecological gifts, what does an old-growth forest offer to the human heart and mind? Science is not set up to answer that question—but art may be. Five years ago, the Spring Creek Project at Oregon State University, in collaboration with the Andrews Forest Long Term Ecological Research Group, began inviting a series of writers to spend week-long residencies here in order to provide ways of observing the land that might complement the ways of science. Writers' responses—poems, stories, essays, field notes, journals—will be added to the stream of instrument data, technical reports, scientific papers, aerial photographs, statistics, and maps, to give a more comprehensive vision of this place. And a vision not only of the present, but of the forest evolving through time, for the sponsors have designed the series of residencies to extend over two centuries.

Designing any human enterprise to last two hundred years may seem brash in an era of headlong haste. Yet precisely because we live in a culture addicted to instant results, such a long-term plan strikes me as visionary and generous, for it seeks to free our thoughts from present needs and to accumulate knowledge that will benefit our descendants. Colleges, museums, and libraries have been founded in the same spirit, to serve the needs not only of the living but also of those not yet born.

Without benefit of planning, the oldest trees in the Andrews have survived since the time of the Crusades, and those along the trail to Lookout Creek have endured since Spaniards first set foot in the New World. These veterans haven't had to contend with wars, religious schisms, economic depressions, regime changes, corrupt government, or the other ills that humans fall prey to, but they have withstood countless natural hazards. And now they must contend with a destabilized climate, a tattered ozone layer, invasive species, and other hazards imposed by humans. At this perilous moment, I have traveled here from Indiana to add my mite of observations to a record that is designed to be kept for generations. I suspect I will come away with far more questions than answers, but that proportion seems in keeping with the spirit of science as well as art.

During my week in the Andrews Forest, each morning at first light I repeat the journey to Lookout Creek, and each time I stop along the way to embrace the same giant Douglas-fir, which smells faintly of moist earth. I wear no watch. I do not hurry. I stay with the tree until it lets me go.

When at length I lean away, I touch my forehead and feel the rough imprint of the bark. I stare up the trunk and spy dawn sky fretted by branches. Perspective makes the tops of the surrounding, smaller trees appear to lean toward this giant one, as if conferring. The cinnamon-colored bark is like a rugged landscape in miniature, with flat ridges separated by deep fissures. Here and there among the fissures, spiderwebs span the gaps. The plates are furred with moss. A skirt of sloughed bark and fallen needles encircles the base of the trunk. Even in the absence of wind, dry needles the color of old pennies rain steadily down, ticking against my jacket.

I don't imagine that my visits mean anything to the Douglas-

fir. I realize it's nonsensical to speak of a tree as patient or generous or dignified merely because it stands there while researchers and children clamber up ropes into its highest limbs. But
how can I know a tree's inwardness? Certainly there is intelligence here, and in the forest as a whole, if by that word we
mean an organism or system responding appropriately to its
circumstances. How does that intelligence compare with ours?
What can we learn from it? And why, out of the many giants
thriving here, does this one draw me to an embrace?

The only intelligence I can examine directly is my own and,
indirectly, that of my species. We are a contradictory lot. Our
indifference to other species, and even to our own long-term
well-being, is demonstrated everywhere one looks, from the
depleted oceans to the heating atmosphere, from poisoned wetlands to eroding farmlands and forests killed by acid rain. Who
can bear in mind this worldwide devastation and the swelling
catalog of extinctions without grieving? And yet it's equally
clear that we are capable of feeling sympathy, curiosity, and
even love toward other species and toward the Earth. Where
does this impulse come from, this sense of affiliation with rivers
and ravens, mountains and mosses? How might it be nurtured?
What role might it play in moving us to behave more caringly
on this beleaguered planet?

These are the questions I find myself brooding about as I
sit in meditation beside Lookout Creek. One is not supposed to
brood while meditating, of course, so again and again I let go of
thoughts and return my awareness to the water sounds, the radi-
ant autumn leaves, the wind on my cheek, the stony cold chill-
ing my sitting bones. And each morning, for shorter or longer
spells, the fretful *I* quiets down, turns transparent, vanishes.

Eventually I stir, roused by the haggle of ravens or the chat-
ter of squirrels or the scurry of deer—other minds in the forest—

and I make my way back along the trail to the zone of electricity and words.

In the evenings I consult field guides to learn the names of organisms that have captivated me here. The pale green, wispy lichen that dangles from branches is known as old man's beard and belongs to the genus *Usnea*. It contains potent antibiotics, a fact understood by Native Americans, who used it to staunch wounds. The flat lichen that grows on top of limbs is *Lobaria oregana*, commonly called "lettuce lichen" or "frog skin lichen"; it fixes nitrogen from the air and thereby enriches the soil when it tumbles to the forest floor. Pacific yew (*Taxus brevifolia*), which grows hunched and gnarled in the understory, is the source of a medicine now widely used in treating cancer. Noble fir (*Abies procera*), favored as a Christmas tree, prefers higher altitudes. Douglas-fir (*Pseudotsuga menziesii*) is not a true fir, and Western red cedar (*Thuja plicata*) is not a true cedar. And the Western hemlock (*Tsuga heterophylla*) bears no relation to the European hemlock, whose poison put a famous end to the life of Socrates.

When I return to my Indiana home, I will write up my Andrews reflections before a window that looks out on an Eastern hemlock (*Tsuga canadensis*), which for thirty-five years now has been a shaggy companion to my shaggy thoughts.

At midday, sunlight floods the gravel bar on Lookout Creek, illuminating strands of spider filament that curve from one boulder to another over an expanse of rushing water. I can't fathom how spiders managed this engineering feat. The wind might have blown them one direction but not back again, yet at least a dozen gossamer threads zigzag between the massive stones.

Against a halcyon blue sky, the spires of trees stand out with startling clarity, their fringe of lichens appearing incandescent.

Moths and gnats flutter above the stream, chased by dragon-flies. The creek is lined by drift logs in various states of decay, from bone-gray hulks to rotting red lumps. Wet boulders gleam as if lit from within. Cobbles jammed against one another look like the heads of a crowd easing downstream. The muscular current, twisting over rocks, catches and tosses the light. The banks on either side blaze with the salmon-pink leaves of dog-woods, those western relatives of the beloved understory tree of my Indiana forests. Everything I see is exquisite—the stones of all sizes laid against one another just so, the perforated leaves of red alders, the fallen needles gathered in pockets along the shore, the bending grasses, the soaring trees.

Can all this reaching for sunlight, nutrients, and water mean nothing? And if it means something, what does it mean, and to whom? What power draws the elements together and binds them into a fern or a forest? If we answer, "Life," we give only a name, not an explanation.

One afternoon, I stroll down the entrance road from the for-est headquarters toward the mouth of Lookout Creek, where it empties into the Blue River. The murmur of water accompanies me the whole way. The air is still, yet butter-yellow maple leaves come sashaying down, littering the pavement. A pewter sheen glints from the bark of young Douglas-firs, which is surpris-ingly light in color, almost like aspen or gray birch.

At the bottom of the slope I pause on a bridge that leads across the Blue River into a National Forest campground, which is closed for the season. In summer, with the floodgates shut in a dam south of here, the river would be backed up into a reser-voir, but now, in October, the water curls unobstructed through bedrock as knobby and gray as elephant hide. The streamside terraces look as green and trim as well-kept pasture. The spacious view of sky and river and mountains cheers me, and helps me understand the sense of oppression our ancestors felt in the deep, dark, dank woods.

In the deserted campground, a bulletin board carries a warning about invasive plants and a notice about a local woman who has been missing since August. I recall this notice a few minutes later when, crossing back over the bridge, I find on the railing a woman's high-heeled sandal, size 7. The toe-strap and three-inch heel are made of clear plastic impregnated with glitter. Bold letters on the insole spell out the brand, which reads like a slogan: NO BOUNDARIES. The bottom of the shoe identifies the model as "Cinderella" and the place of manufacture as China. Bemused, I start spinning a story that would bring this fairy-tale object from Asia to a forest road in Oregon.

A roaring distracts me, and I look up to see a red pickup hurtle by carrying a mud-spattered four-wheeler—another expression of the No Boundaries creed.

As I climb the hill, I think about how we impose our machines and schemes everywhere, in the atmosphere and oceans and on every acre of ground, including the Andrews Experimental Forest. Off-road joy riders, National Park snowmobilers, wilderness oil-drillers, factory boat trawlers, 24/7 merchants, cornucopian economists—all deny the notion of limits. But without limits we cannot have ethics, which require us to accept boundaries, to refrain from certain actions, to distinguish between what is possible and what is right.

Then what about our compulsion to find human stories in nature? Isn't that another defiance of boundaries? We envision bears and hunters and wandering sisters in the stars. We spy dragons in the shapes of clouds, hear mournfulness in the calls of owls. Reason tells us that such analogies are false. For all its delicious sounds, the creek does not speak, but merely slides downhill, taking the path of least resistance, rubbing against whatever it meets along the way. Bedrock is not elephant hide, lichens are not horsetails, moss is not fur, spiders are not engineers, ravens do not haggle, and trees do not confer. Scientists are schooled to avoid such anthropomorphism. Writers are warned against committing the "pathetic fallacy," which is the error of projecting human emotions or meanings onto nature. But if we forgo such analogies, if we withhold our stories, we estrange ourselves from the universe. We become mere onlookers, the sole meaning-bearing witnesses of a meaningless show. So can I uphold the necessity of constraints on human actions, while denying such constraints on thought?

Those who fancy themselves separate from nature often use "tree-hugger" as a term of ridicule, as if to feel the allure of trees were a perverted form of sensuality or a throwback to our simian ancestry. Of course, many who decry tree-hugging don't believe we *have* a simian ancestry, so perhaps what they fear is a reversion to paganism. And they may have a point. The religions that started in the Middle East—Judaism, Christianity, Islam—are all desert faiths, created by people who lived in the open. Theirs is a sky god, who would be eclipsed by a forest canopy. In every civilization influenced by these faiths, trees have been cut down not merely to secure wood for cooking and building or to clear ground for agriculture or to open vistas around settlements where predators might lurk, but to reveal the heavens.

Worship of a sky god has been costly to our planet. Religions that oppose the heavenly to the earthly, elevating the former and denigrating the latter, are in effect denying that we emerge from and wholly depend on nature. If you think of the touchable, eatable, climbable, sexy, singing, material world as fallen, corrupt, and sinful, then you are likely to abuse it. You are likely to say that we might as well cut down the last old-growth forests, drain the last swamps, catch the last tuna and cod, burn the last drops of oil, since the end time is coming, when the elect few will be raptured away to the immortal realm of spirit, and everything earthy will be utterly erased.

But our language preserves a countervailing wisdom. In Latin, *materia* means stuff, anything substantial, and in particular it means wood. *Materia* in turn derives from *mater*, which means mother. In the collective imagination that gave rise to these meanings, trees were understood to epitomize matter, and matter was understood to be life-giving. Perhaps we could tap into this wisdom by recovering another word that derives from *mater*—*matrix*, which means "womb." Instead of speaking about "nature" or "the environment," terms that imply some realm apart from us, perhaps we should speak of Earth as our matrix, our mother, the source and sustainer of life.

One morning beside Lookout Creek, enveloped as usual in watery music, I sit leaning against a young red alder that has sprouted in the gravel bar, its leaves nibbled into lace by insects. Everything here either starts as food or winds up as food. None of the alders growing on this ever-shifting bank are thicker than a baseball bat. The next big flood will scour them away. Beside me, the sinewy roots of an upturned stump seem to mimic the muscular current in the stream. The bar is littered with gray and ruddy stones pockmarked by holes that betray the volcanic origins of this rubble.

Where better than such a place to recognize that the essence of nature is *flow*—of lava, electrons, water, wind, breath. *Materia*, matter, the seemingly solid stuff we encounter—trees, stones, bears, bones—is actually fluid, constantly changing, like water shapes in the current. The Psalmist tells us, "The mountains skipped like rams, and the little hills like lambs," and Dōgen, a thirteenth-century Zen teacher, proclaims that mountains are always walking. Both speak truly. Mountains do move, arising and eroding away over geological time, just as organisms grow and decay, species evolve, tectonic plates shift, stars congeal and burn and expire, entire galaxies shine for a spell and then vanish. Nothing in nature is fixed.

Conservationists have often been accused of wishing to freeze the land in some favored condition—for example, the American continent as it was before European colonization. Back when maps described old growth as large saw-timber, scientists spoke of forests reaching climax, as if at some point the flow would cease. But we now realize that no such stasis is possible, even if it were desirable. If flux is the nature of nature, however, we still must make distinctions among the *kinds* of change. We cannot resist the damage caused by human behavior unless we distinguish between *natural* change—for example, the long history of extinctions—and *anthropogenic* change—for example, the recent acceleration in extinctions due to habitat destruction, pollution, climate heating, and other disturbances caused by humans. The capacity to make such a distinction, and to act on it, may be as distinctive of our species as the capacity to use symbolic language.

Thoughts flow, along with everything else, even in the depths of meditation. And yet the human mind seems compelled to imagine fixity—heaven, nirvana, Plato's ideal realm, eternal God—and the human heart yearns for permanence. Why else do we treasure diamonds and gold? Why else do Creationists cling to the notion that all species were made in exactly their present form? Why else do we search for scientific "laws" underlying the constant flux of the universe?

Our yearning for the fixed, like our craving for dominion over nature, may be another expression of our fear of aging and death. This occurs to me as I sit, transfixed, beside the narrowest, noisiest passage in the riffles on Lookout Creek. A dozen dead snags tilt above my head, their bare limbs like the sparse whiskers on an old man's chin. Upstream, a gigantic Douglas-fir has fallen across the creek, its trunk still as straight as when it was alive. Just downstream, another giant has fallen, this one snapped in the middle. I can't help imagining one of the looming snags suddenly toppling onto me and snapping my thread of thought, scattering this temporary congregation of elements and notions bearing my name.

Higher up the valley of Lookout Creek, in a grove of five-hundred-year-old Douglas-firs and Western hemlocks, a hundred or so logs have been placed side by side on the ground, labeled with aluminum tags, and fitted with instruments to measure their rate and manner of decay. This is one of six so-called "log decomposition sites" in the Andrews, part of another experiment designed to continue for two hundred years. This research aims to document, among other things, the role of dead wood in forest ecology and in the sequestering of carbon.

On my visits to the site, I stroke the moss-covered logs, touch the rubbery fungi that sprout from every surface, peer into the boxy traps that catch flying insects and fallen debris, and lean close to the tubes that capture the logs' exhalations. The only breathing I detect is my own. I'm intrigued that scientists are studying decomposition, for as an artist I usually think about *composition*—the making of something shapely and whole out of elements. A musician composes with notes, a painter with colors, a writer with letters and words, much as life orchestrates carbon, oxygen, nitrogen, and other ingredients into organisms.

These organisms—trees, fungi, ravens, humans—persist for a while, change over time, and eventually dissolve back into their constituents, which will be gathered up again into living things.

Art and life both draw energy from sunlight, directly or indirectly, to counter entropy by increasing order. Right now, for example, I'm running on the secondhand sunshine bound up in pancakes and maple syrup. Organisms interact biophysically with everything in their ecosystem, and ultimately with the whole universe. By contrast, the symbolic structures that humans create—songs, stories, poems, paintings, photographs, films, diagrams, mathematical formulas, computer codes—convey influence only insofar as they are read, heard, or otherwise perceived by humans. What happens when we turn our interpretive powers on living organisms? Does raven, Douglas-fir, spider, or lichen mean anything different, or anything more, when it is taken up into human consciousness?

What we think or imagine about other species clearly influences our behavior toward them—as notions about the wickedness of wolves led to their extermination throughout much of their historical range, and as new understanding about the role of predators has led to the reintroduction of wolves in Yellowstone and elsewhere. But aside from this practical impact, does our peculiar sort of mind bear any greater significance in the scheme of things? Is it merely an accidental result of mechanical processes, an adaptive feature that has powered our—perhaps fleeting—evolutionary success? Would the universe lose anything vital if our species suddenly vanished?

We can't know the answer to those questions, despite the arguments of prophets and philosophers. We can only form hunches, and, right or wrong, these will influence the spirit of our work and the tenor of our lives. For what it's worth, my hunch is that what we call mind is not a mere side effect of material evolution, but is fundamental to reality. It is not separate from what we call matter, but is a revelation of the inwardness of things. I suspect that our symbol-wielding intelligence is a manifestation of the creative, shaping energy that drives the cosmos, from the dance of electrons to the growth of trees. If this is so, then our highest calling may be to composition—paying attention to some portion of the world, reflecting on what we have perceived, and fashioning a response in words or numbers or paint or song or some other expressive medium. Our paintings on cave walls, our photos of quasars, our graphs and sonnets and songs may be the gifts we return for the privilege of sojourning here on this marvelous globe.

If intelligence means the ability to take in and respond to information, then all organisms possess it, whether plant or animal, for they constantly exchange signals and materials with their surroundings. If intelligence means the capacity for solving puzzles or using language, then surely the ravens that clamor above me or the wolves that roam the far side of the mountains possess it. But if we are concerned with the power not merely to reason or use language, but to discern and define meanings, to evaluate actions in light of ethical principles, to pass on knowledge across generations through symbolic forms—then we are speaking about a kind of intelligence that appears to be the exclusive power of humans, at least on this planet.

Some contemplative traditions maintain that this meaning-making capacity is a curse, that it divorces us from reality, enclosing us in a bubble of abstractions. It's easy to sympathize with this view when one considers our history of feuds and frauds. Cleverness alone does not make us wise. Yet here among these great trees and boisterous mountain streams, I sense that our peculiar sort of mind might also be a blessing, not only to us but to the forest, to other creatures, to life on Earth, and even to the universe.

I recognize the danger of hubris. It's flattering to suppose, as most religions do, that humans occupy a unique place in the order of things. The appeal of an idea is not evidence for its falsity, however, but merely a reason for caution. Cautiously, therefore: Suppose that the universe is not a machine, as nineteenth-century science claimed, but rather a field of energy, as twentieth-century science imagined. Suppose that mind is not some private power that each of us contains, but rather an energy field that contains us—and likewise encompasses birds, bees, ferns, trees, salamanders, spiders, dragonflies, and all living things, each kind offering its own degree and variety of awareness. What if our role in this all-embracing mind is to gaze back at the grand matrix that birthed us, and translate our responses into symbolic expression? What if science and literature, painting and mathematics, photography and music and dance and our many other modes of expression feed back into the encompassing mind? And if that is our distinctive role, how should we lead our lives?

After communing with the great Douglas-fir one last time, I pack my bag, load the rental car, and set off along a forest road flanked by the looming presences of trees, on the first leg of my return trip to Indiana. As I drive, it occurs to me that meditation is an effort to become for a spell more like a tree, open to whatever arises, without judging, without remembering the past or anticipating the future, fully present in the moment. The taste of that stillness during my stay at the Andrews Forest has refreshed me. And yet I do not aspire to dwell in such a condition always. For all its grandeur and beauty, for all its half-millennium longevity, the Douglas-fir cannot bear me in mind, cannot reflect or remember or imagine—can only *be*. Insofar as meditation returns us to that state of pure, unreflective being, it is a respite from the burden of ceaseless thought. When we surface from meditation, however, we are not turning from reality to illusion, as some spiritual traditions would have us believe; rather, we are reclaiming the full powers of mind, renewed by our immersion in the realm of mountains and rivers, wind and breath.

Contributors

ROBERT AITKEN was, until his recent death at the age of ninety-three, a master of the Diamond Sangha, a Zen Buddhist society he cofounded with his wife. One of the elders of Zen Buddhism in North America, a voice for socially engaged spirituality, and the author of more than ten books, including *Taking the Path of Zen, The Mind of Clover,* and *Zen Master Raven,* he was a lifetime resident of Hawai'i.

JOHN ANDERSON grew up in Britain, New Zealand, and California and currently holds the William H. Drury, Jr., Chair in Evolution, Ecology, and Natural History at College of the Atlantic in Bar Harbor, Maine, where he has taught for over twenty years. He has studied marine birds and the relationship between cultural history and ecological patterns on Maine's coastal islands throughout this time. He recently served as President of the Society for Human Ecology, and as Chair of the Human Ecology Section of the Ecological Society of America.

PAUL DAYTON has been on the faculty of the Scripps Institution of Oceanography for almost four decades, conducting research on marine ecosystems throughout the world—including kelp forests, rocky intertidal communities, and Antarctic benthic communities. He has served on numerous scientific advisory boards and received many awards and honors, including the E. O. Wilson Naturalist Award from the American Society of Naturalists and a Lifetime Achievement Award from the Western

Society of Naturalists, and he is the only person ever to be awarded both the Mercer and Cooper awards from the Ecological Society of America.

ALISON HAWTHORNE DEMING, Professor of Creative Writing at the University of Arizona, has written four books of poetry, most recently *Rope*, and three books of creative nonfiction. She is the recipient of numerous fellowships and awards, including the Walt Whitman Award of the Academy of American Poets. Her work often explores the boundary between artistic and scientific ways of viewing the world.

CRISTINA EISENBERG is a conservation biologist and nature writer who lives in northwestern Montana, where she studies wolves and other carnivores on both sides of the international border. She is a doctoral candidate at Oregon State University, where she has received many honors for her work, including a Boone and Crocket Fellowship. She is the author of *The Wolf's Tooth: Keystone Predators, Trophic Cascades, and Biodiversity*.

WREN FARRIS divides her time between the Oregon coast and the desert Southwest. In Oregon she works on turning plastic pollution from the ocean into large-scale educational art, and in New Mexico she continues to build an off-grid straw-bale house. Wren worked in communications and conference production for many years for Bioneers and has helped found three environmental nonprofits. She is currently the managing director of Artula Institute for Arts and Environmental Education. Her writing, which explores the connections between landscapes, poetics, and human relationship to place, has appeared in *Orion*, *Mountain Gazette*, and other periodicals.

THOMAS LOWE FLEISCHNER is a naturalist, conservation biologist, and teacher. Author of two books—*Singing Stone: A Natural History of the Escalante Canyons* and *Desert Wetlands*—and numerous articles, he has taught in the interdisciplinary environmental studies program at Prescott College, in Arizona, for over two decades. Cofounder of the North Cascades Institute, and founding President of the Natural History Network, he has served on the Board of Governors of the Society for Conservation Biology and as President of its Colorado Plateau Chapter.

DAVE FOREMAN is a wilderness and conservation visionary, as well as the author of several books, including *Rewilding North America, Confes-*

sions of an Eco-Warrior, and the eco-thriller *The Lobo Outback Funeral Home.* After working many years for The Wilderness Society, he was co-founder of the Earth First! movement and publisher of *Wild Earth,* and he now serves as founding Executive Director of the Rewilding Institute, based in New Mexico.

CHARLES GOODRICH is a poet and essayist who worked as a profes-sional gardener for twenty-five years. Charles is the author of two collec-tions of poems, *Going to Seed: Dispatches from the Garden* and *Insects of South Corvallis;* a book of essays, *The Practice of Home;* and coeditor of *In the Blast Zone: Catastrophe and Renewal on Mount St. Helens.* He is the Program Director of the Spring Creek Project for Ideas, Nature, and the Written Word at Oregon State University.

R. EDWARD GRUMBINE was Director of the Sierra Institute wilderness studies field program at the University of California, Santa Cruz, for two decades, and now teaches environmental studies at Prescott College in Arizona. Currently a research fellow at the Kunming Institute of Botany in Yunnan, China, he is the author of *Where the Dragon Meets the Angry River: Nature and Power in the People's Republic of China* and *Ghost Bears: Exploring the Biodiversity Crisis* and the editor of *Environmental Policy and Biodiversity.*

JANE HIRSHFIELD is the author of seven books of poetry, including *After* and the forthcoming *Come, Thief.* Her collection of essays, *Nine Gates: Entering the Mind of Poetry* is considered a classic in the field. She has also edited and cotranslated three books collecting the work of women poets from the past. Her awards include fellowships from the Guggenheim and Rockefeller foundations, the National Endowment for the Arts, and the Academy of American Poets; multiple appearances in the *Best American Poetry* series; the Poetry Center Book Award; the California Book Award; and finalist status for both the National Book Critics Circle Award and England's T. S. Eliot Prize in Poetry. She lives in northern California.

ROBIN WALL KIMMERER teaches botany and forest ecology at the State University of New York College of Environmental Science and Forestry, where she is also the Director of the Center for Native Peoples and the Environment. Her work attempts to integrate traditional ecological knowledge of indigenous peoples with perspectives from contemporary biological sciences. Of Potawatomi descent, she is the author of *Gathering Moss: A Natural and Cultural History of Mosses*, for which she was awarded the John Burroughs Medal for outstanding nature writing.

KEN LAMBERTON has written five books, including *Wilderness and Razor Wire*, an account of his relationship with nature while in prison, which won the John Burroughs Medal for outstanding nature writing. He has also authored more than a hundred articles and essays and was included in the anthology *The Best American Science and Nature Writing 2000*. He lives in southern Arizona.

ROBERT MACFARLANE is a Fellow in English Literature at Cambridge University in Great Britain. Among his many writings are two books, *Mountains of the Mind: A History of a Fascination* and *The Wild Places*, both of which have won multiple awards and were filmed by the BBC. He also frequently writes on literature, travel, and the environment for many publications in Britain and North America.

KATHLEEN DEAN MOORE is an essayist, activist, parent, and Distinguished Professor of Philosophy and University Writer Laureate at Oregon State University. She is the author of *Riverwalking: Reflections on Moving Water*, *Holdfast: At Home in the Natural World*, *The Pine Island Paradox*, and *Wild Comfort: A Book of Healing*, as well as academic textbooks on moral philosophy. These books have won the Pacific Northwest Booksellers' Award, the Sigurd Olson Nature Writing Award, and the Outstanding Academic Book Award.

ROBERT MICHAEL PYLE writes essay, poetry, and fiction along a tributary of the Lower Columbia River. His fifteen books include *Wintergreen*, *The Thunder Tree*, *Walking the High Ridge: Life as Field Trip*, and a definitive field guide, *The Butterflies of Cascadia*. His 2008 travels across America, net in hand, are chronicled in his latest book, *Mariposa Road: The First Butterfly Big Year*. A Guggenheim Fellow, he has received the John Burroughs Medal, the National Outdoor Book Award, and the Distinguished Service Award from the Society for Conservation Biology. He has taught for the Aga Khan Trust for the Humanities in Tajikistan, as Kittredge Visiting Writer at the University of Montana, and in many other settings.

SARAH JUNIPER RABKIN is a writer, editor, and visual artist with a background in science journalism. She grew up in Berkeley, California, in the 1960s and 1970s, and now lives near Monterey Bay with her husband, poet Charles Atkinson. A longtime teacher of writing and environmental studies at the University of California, Santa Cruz, she also leads outdoor workshops on keeping illustrated field journals.

SCOTT RUSSELL SANDERS, Distinguished Professor Emeritus of English at Indiana University, is the author of more than twenty books of fiction and nonfiction, including *A Private History of Awe*, which was nominated for the Pulitzer Prize, and *A Conservationist Manifesto*. His work—which explores relationships between nature and culture, social justice and spirituality, and dignity and honest work—has garnered many awards and fellowships, including a Lannan Literary Award and the Mark Twain Award.

LAURA SEWALL is an ecopsychologist and conservationist living on the coast of Maine, where she serves as the Director of the Bates-Morse Mountain Conservation Area and the Bates College Coastal Center at Shortridge. Laura holds a master's degree in environmental law from the Vermont Law School and a PhD in visual science from Brown University. She is the author of *Sight and Sensibility: The Ecopsychology of Perception*.

JOHN TALLMADGE is a literary and educational consultant based in Cincinnati, Ohio. A past president of the Association for the Study of Literature and Environment, he has served on the faculties of the Union Institute, Carleton College, and the University of Utah. He is the author of *Meeting the Tree of Life: A Teacher's Path* and *The Cincinnati Arch: Learning from Nature in the City* as well as numerous essays on nature, culture, and environmental literature.

RICHARD THOMPSON, proclaimed "one of the finest guitarists on Earth" (*All Music Guide to Rock*) and among the twenty "greatest guitarists of all time" (*Rolling Stone*), and recipient of a BBC Lifetime Achievement Award, was one of the founding members of the seminal British folk-rock group Fairport Convention, collaborated with his then-wife, Linda Thompson, and has been a solo recording artist for the past three decades. A gifted songwriter, his songs have been recorded by many other artists, including Bonnie Raitt, Elvis Costello, and David Byrne.

STEPHEN C. TROMBULAK is Professor of Environmental and Biosphere Studies and Director of the Conservation Biology Laboratory at Middlebury College in Middlebury, Vermont. A vertebrate biologist and dedicated naturalist, he has served as Chair of the Education Committee of the Society for Conservation Biology, and President of its North American Section. He is the founding editor of the *Journal of Natural History Education and Experience* and a member of the board of the Natural History Network.